ESSENTIAL MONEY SKILLS FOR TEENS

THE ULTIMATE GUIDE TO MASTERING A BUDGET, NAVIGATING BANKING, UNDERSTANDING SAVINGS AND INVESTMENTS, MANAGING CREDIT, PLANNING FOR COLLEGE, AND THRIVING FINANCIALLY!

JORDAN WIZE

CONTENTS

To Camden and Hadley,

In every page of this journey, in every line of wisdom, and in every piece of advice, you'll find echoes of hope, resilience, and the endless possibilities that await you. May this book be a guiding light on your path, a compass in your hands, and a reminder that your dreams, no matter how vast, are within reach.

With every challenge you overcome and every success you celebrate, know that you are the inspiration behind these words. This book is dedicated to you, for in your hearts lies the courage to dream and the power to achieve.

May you always navigate the seas of life with the same curiosity and bravery that fill your spirits now. Here's to your journey, your discoveries, and the wonderful story you will write in the world.

With all my love and endless belief in your potential, Jordan

INTRODUCTION - NAVIGATING THE MONETARY SEAS

Ahoy, young explorers! Welcome the next leg of our voyage as we explore money and finance. Imagine money as the vast ocean upon which all of us set sail. Its waves and tides can carry us to distant shores of opportunity or leave us stranded on isles of economic uncertainty. The truth is as clear as a bell on a crisp morning at sea: understanding money is like knowing the art of seafaring in an ever-changing world.

In the vast American seascape, 60% of teen sailors have yet to chart the waters of basic financial navigation. It's a bewildering statistic that exists not for lack of maps but for lack of compasses. Schools often leave the compass rose of personal finance unexplored, and it's high time we plot a new course.

I can think back to when I was a young mariner, much like you, navigating from the simple coves of pocket money to the expansive bays of paychecks. My voyage was fraught with missteps and the occasional storm of mismanaged funds. I wished for a seasoned captain to steer me through the fog of financial jargon and into the clear.

This book is my message in a bottle to you, sent across the waters of experience. It's a trove of practical wisdom—a guide to the hidden reefs and bountiful ports that await. Within these pages lie tales of commerce and coins, a collection of nautical charts for the modern world of money.

Together, we will trim the sails of budgeting and chart the stars of credit. We'll decipher the economy's language and the stock market's signals. Each lesson is a nautical mile on your journey to financial literacy.

As the captain of your ship, you're about to embark on a most crucial quest—gaining the confidence to sail the monetary seas with insight and agility. From the still waters of saving to the gale-force winds of investing, I'll help you navigate it all.

So, batten down the hatches and raise the anchor. Your adventure into financial literacy awaits; with each new chapter, we'll sail closer to the horizon of independence. Are you ready to steer your course into the waters of wealth and wisdom? Then, my brave voyager, let us chart this journey together!

CHAPTER ONE

DECODING YOUR PAYCHECK

1.1 UNDERSTANDING GROSS VS. NET PAY

Gross Pay: The Starting Point

Think of your gross pay as a big, juicy apple straight off the tree. It's the total amount of money you've earned before anything has been subtracted. If you're paid hourly, it's calculated by multiplying the hours you've worked by your hourly wage. If you're on a salary, it's your annual salary divided by the number of pay periods in a year.

Net Pay: The Apple after a Few Bites

Now, imagine taking a few bites out of that apple. What's left is still an apple, but it's a little smaller than when you started. That's what your net pay is like. It's the amount of money you take home after various deductions have been taken out of your gross pay. These deductions include taxes, retirement contributions, and health insurance premiums. Your net pay is the amount that ends up in your pocket (or your bank account) for you to spend.

The Difference between Gross and Net Pay

So, the difference between gross and net pay is caused by the deductions taken from your paycheck. But why do these deductions occur? It's a combination of legal obligations and benefits for you.

Let's put it this way. Imagine you and your friends decide to start a band, and you have your first gig. The money you all earn from the gig is like your gross pay. But then you have to pay for gas for the van, a new guitar string that broke during the performance, and a pizza to celebrate your first show. After these expenses (or deductions), the money left to divide between you is like your net pay. It's what you get to take home and spend after meeting necessary expenses.

How Taxes and Deductions Affect Your Paycheck

One of the primary deductions from your gross pay is taxes. Depending on where you live, you could have federal, state, and even local taxes taken out of your paycheck. These taxes fund things like schools, roads, and public services that we all use.

Other standard deductions include Social Security and Medicare taxes. These programs provide benefits for retirees, people with disabilities, and children of deceased workers. When you pay into these programs, you're helping to support these individuals, and one day, when you retire, you'll receive these benefits, too.

You may also have deductions for benefits you've chosen to participate in, such as health insurance or a retirement savings plan like a 401(k). While it can be challenging to see your gross pay shrink, these deductions work for your benefit, providing healthcare coverage and helping you save for the future.

Reading Your Pay Stub

A pay stub is a document that details your earnings and deductions for a specific pay period. It's like a receipt for your work. On the stub, you'll see your gross pay listed at the top, followed by deductions. After subtracting all the deductions, you'll see your net pay at the bottom.

Reviewing your pay stub after each pay period is an excellent habit to get into. It lets you see exactly where your money is going and ensures no errors. Feel free to ask your employer if you see a deduction you need help understanding or if your net pay seems lower than it should be. It's your money, after all, and you have a right to know where it's going.

So, the next time you get your paycheck, don't just glance at the net pay and toss the pay stub aside. Take a few minutes to review the details. Understanding your gross vs. net pay is crucial to being financially savvy. After all, it's not just about how much you make; it's also about knowing where it's going.

Now that we've tackled the difference between gross and net pay let's dive into the details of those deductions. Next, we'll demystify the world of tax deductions and explain how they affect your paycheck. But that's a topic for the next section. For now, give yourself a pat on the back. You've taken your first step toward understanding your paycheck. Well done!

1.2 THE MYSTERY OF TAX DEDUCTIONS

Let's move onto a topic that tends to make people's eyes glaze over tax deductions. It sounds like a snooze fest but stick with me here. Understanding these deductions is like cracking a secret code that can help you manage your money better. So, let's put on our detective hats and start unraveling this mystery.

Common Types of Tax Deductions

You'll find that taxes make up a significant part of the deductions on your pay stub. These include federal income tax, state income tax (if your state has one), Social Security tax, and Medicare tax. Each of these serves a specific purpose.

The government uses federal and state income taxes to fund education, infrastructure, and defense services. The Social Security tax funds a program that provides benefits to retirees and disabled individuals, while the Medicare tax supports a healthcare program for seniors.

I get it. Seeing these deductions on your paycheck can feel like a bummer. But remember, they're not just disappearing into a black hole. These taxes contribute to services and programs that benefit you, your family, and your community.

Why Taxes Are Deducted from Your Paycheck

You might be wondering why these taxes are deducted from your paycheck in the first place. Why not pay them all at once at the end of the year? The system of taking taxes out of each paycheck, known as withholding, is designed to make it easier to pay your taxes by paying them gradually rather than in one lump sum.

Think of it like ordering a pizza with your friends. Instead of one person footing the bill and waiting for everyone to pay them back, each person contributes their share upfront. It's more manageable, there's less risk of someone forgetting to pay, and there's no big, scary bill waiting at the end.

The Role of W-4 Forms in Tax Deductions

So, how does your employer know how much tax to withhold from your paycheck? That's where the W-4 form comes into play. When you start a new job, one of the many papers you'll fill out is a W-4 form. This form determines the tax amount to be withheld from your paycheck.

On the W-4, you'll provide some basic information about your tax situation, such as whether you're married and how many jobs you have. You'll also claim allowances, essentially deductions that reduce the amount of your pay subject to tax.

The more allowances you claim, the less tax will be withheld from your paycheck. It's tempting to claim many allowances to keep more money in your pocket now, but be careful. If you claim too many allowances and need more tax withheld, you could owe money when you file your tax return.

On the flip side, if you claim too few allowances, too much tax will be withheld, and you'll get a refund when you file your tax return. A refund might sound nice, but it essentially means you've given the government an interest-free loan with your money.

The goal is to get your withholding close to your actual tax liability. That way, you're not giving up too much of your paycheck throughout the year, but you're also not hit with a big tax bill at the end of the year. If something changes your life situation, like getting married or having a baby, you can fill out a new W-4 to adjust your withholding.

There you have it! The mystery of tax deductions is solved. By understanding these deductions, you're gaining more control over your money and taking another step toward financial literacy. But remember, this is just one piece of the puzzle. Next, we'll discuss other deductions on your paycheck, like health benefits and retirement contributions. But that's a topic for the future. For now, take a moment to celebrate your newfound knowledge of tax deductions. Please give yourself a high five; you've earned it!

1.3 THE PERKS: HEALTH BENEFITS AND RETIREMENT CONTRIBUTIONS

Let's shift our focus from the mandatory deductions on your paycheck to something more exciting - the perks! Yes, you read that right. While the word 'deduction' might make you cringe, some deductions are more akin to benefits. Depending on your employer, these include health insurance contributions, retirement savings, life insurance, and potentially more.

Understanding Health Insurance Deductions

First, let's talk about health insurance. If you're enrolled in a health insurance plan through your employer, the premium for that insurance is typically deducted from your paycheck. This deduction is an automatic way to pay for your health coverage. When you visit a doctor, hospital, or pharmacy, your health insurance helps cover those costs, which can be pretty hefty without coverage.

Remember that health insurance is an investment in your well-being. You might be young and healthy now, but unexpected health issues can crop up anytime. Health insurance gives you peace of mind, knowing you're financially protected in a medical emergency. So, view that health insurance deduction as a small price to pay for a whole lot of security.

The Basics of Retirement Contributions Like a 401(k)

Next on the list is retirement contributions. Wait, retirement? I know, I know. Retirement can seem like a lifetime away when starting your professional journey. But trust me on this: creating your retirement savings at a young age is one of the smartest financial moves you can make.

If your employer offers a retirement plan like a 401(k), you can contribute a portion of your paycheck to this plan. Your contribution money is deducted from your paycheck before taxes, lowering your taxable income. Plus, your 401(k) money grows tax-free until you withdraw it in retirement.

Some employers even offer a match, meaning they will contribute an equal amount to your 401(k) up to a certain percentage of your salary. That's free money towards your retirement! So, while it might be tempting to keep that extra money in your paycheck now, remember that every dollar you put into your retirement fund is a step towards a secure and comfortable retirement.

Other Potential Benefits: Life Insurance and Disability Insurance

Lastly, let's touch on other potential benefits you might see as deductions on your paycheck. Some employers offer life insurance as a benefit to their employees. If you participate, your employer will deduct these premiums from your paycheck. Life insurance provides a financial safety net for your loved ones in the event of your death.

Disability insurance is another potential benefit. This insurance provides you with a portion of your income if you cannot work due to a disability. As with life and health insurance, the premiums for disability insurance are usually deducted directly from your paycheck.

Remember, these benefits are part of your overall compensation package. While they might reduce your take-home pay now, they provide you with valuable protection and financial security. Think of these deductions as you paying yourself in the future- a future where you're covered in case of a health issue, a future where you can retire comfortably, and a future where your loved ones are financially protected.

Alright, you've now cracked the code of your paycheck deductions, but we still have more to discuss. Next, we'll look at how to set up direct deposits so your hard-earned money lands safely in your bank account. For now, take a moment to appreciate the knowledge you've gained. You're becoming a pro at understanding your paycheck, and that's something to be proud of!

1.4 MAKING SENSE OF DIRECT DEPOSITS

Setting up Direct Deposit with Your Employer

So, how do you ensure that your well-earned money lands safely in your bank account? Enter the world of direct deposits. These electronic payments go straight from your employer's bank account to yours. No more waiting for checks to arrive in the mail or making a trip to the bank to deposit them. It's all done automatically.

Setting up direct deposit is as simple as providing your employer with your bank account number and the bank's routing number. These numbers are on checks you may have received when you opened your bank account. The other option is to log in to your bank account online. You can find the information there. You'll also need to specify whether you want your money deposited into your checking or savings account. Once set up, your paycheck will be deposited into your account each payday, like clockwork.

Tracking Your Income through Bank Statements

Now that your pay is deposited directly into your account, you'll want to track it. This is where your bank statement comes in handy. A bank statement records all transactions in your account over a certain period. It shows deposits, withdrawals, fees charged, and the end balance for the period.

Each time your pay is deposited, it will appear on your bank statement as a credit. By checking your bank statement regularly, you can ensure that your pay has been correctly deposited and track how much you're earning. Also, checking your bank statement can help you spot any unusual transactions that could indicate fraud or identity theft.

You know that bank statements sound like a lot of paper. But don't worry; most banks offer electronic statements, or eStatements, that you can access online or through your bank's mobile app. Online apps save paper and make it easy to check your account whenever you want, wherever you are.

The Benefits of Direct Deposit

Direct deposit has several benefits that make it a wise choice for receiving your pay.

First, it's convenient. Your money is available as soon as it's deposited. No more waiting for checks to arrive or clear. Plus, you don't have to worry about losing a paycheck or having it stolen.

Secondly, direct deposit can help you save money. Some banks waive specific fees or offer other perks if you have your paycheck deposited directly. Plus, if your employer allows you to split your direct deposit between different accounts, you can have a portion of your pay automatically deposited into your savings. Depositing into multiple accounts is a great way to automate your savings and help your money grow.

Finally, direct deposit is reliable. You know exactly when your money will be available, which can help with budgeting and planning. It also means you'll still get paid if you're sick, on vacation, or unable to pick up your check for any reason.

So there you have it. By setting up direct deposit and checking your bank statement, you're taking control of your income and ensuring your money is working for you.

As we wrap up this chapter, remember that understanding your paycheck is more than knowing how much you take home. It's about understanding where your money is going, how it's getting to you, and how to manage it effectively. With each paycheck, you're earning more than just money. You're building your financial future. So, here's to you and your journey toward financial literacy. Keep going; you're doing great!

Ask the Captain

Ahoy, Captain! What's the real difference between gross pay and net pay?

Avast, young sailor! Picture your gross pay as a treasure chest full of gold. It's the total bounty you've earned. But before you can enjoy it, ye must pay yer crew and maintain yer ship. Your net pay is the treasure you get to spend on your adventures!

Captain, why do they take taxes out of my paycheck? Can't I pay them all at once?

Listen well, matey! Taxes are like the dues we pay for sailing on safe seas. They're taken piece by piece from yer treasure to avoid a hefty debt at year's end. It's like sharing the cost of a feast with yer crewmates bit by bit rather than owing a grand sum at once.

How do I make sense of all these deductions on my pay stub, Captain?

Sharpen yer spyglass! Your pay stub is like a map of your treasure. Deductions are the costs for safe passage, like contributing to retirement or health insurance. Please review it carefully to ensure no coins are misplaced.

Captain, should I care about retirement plans like a 401(k) at my age?

Aye, young sailor, start early! Contributing to yer 401(k) is like stowing away gold for a distant voyage. The earlier ye start, the more treasure you'll have when ye retire. Some employers even match yer contributions, doubling yer loot!

What are these health insurance deductions on my paycheck, Captain?

Health insurance is like repairing and maintaining yer ship, lad. Ye might not see the immediate need, but you'll be thankful for the protection when a storm hits. It ensures that unexpected medical costs won't swamp you.

Captain, I'm a bit confused. Why should I set up direct deposit for my paycheck?

Direct deposit is like having a faithful parrot deliver yer gold straight to yer treasure chest. It's swift and secure, and you don't have to worry about losing your hard-earned loot. Plus, it helps you keep a better log of your earnings.

Captain, any advice on how to manage my paycheck better?

Chart your course wisely! Allocate parts of your treasure for different needs: some for daily rations, some for yer ship's upkeep (savings), and some for the crew's welfare (insurance and taxes). The better ye manage yer gold, the smoother yer voyage will be!

The Captain's Guiding Light: Your Paycheck (Key Chapter Takeaways)

1. **Gross vs. Net Pay Explained:** Gross pay is the total earnings before deductions, while net pay is what remains after taxes and other deductions like retirement contributions and health insurance premiums.

2. **The Role of Deductions:** Deductions from your gross pay, including taxes, retirement contributions, and insurance premiums, are essential for legal obligations and personal benefits.

3. **Tax Deductions Decoded:** Taxes, including federal, state, and Social Security, are significant deductions from your paycheck, funding public services and future personal benefits.

4. **Understanding the W-4 Form:** The W-4 form determines how much tax is withheld from your paycheck, based on your marital status, number of jobs, and claimed allowances.

5. **Perks Beyond Pay:** Employer-provided benefits like health insurance, retirement savings (401(k)), life insurance, and disability insurance are valuable, even though they reduce your take-home pay.

6. **Direct Deposit and Financial Management:** Setting up direct deposit ensures your paycheck is securely and promptly deposited into your bank account, aiding in efficient financial management.

7. **Reading Your Pay Stub:** Regularly reviewing your pay stub helps in understanding where your money goes and ensuring accuracy in your earnings and deductions.

8. **The Importance of Tracking Income:** Monitoring bank statements and understanding direct deposit benefits help maintain a clear picture of your financial situation and detect any discrepancies.

9. **The Long-Term View:** Engaging with and understanding your paycheck is crucial for long-term financial literacy, security, and planning for the future.

10. **Empowerment Through Knowledge:** Understanding your paycheck is a significant step towards financial literacy, empowering you to make informed decisions about your earnings and deductions.

CHAPTER TWO

BANKING BASICS: YOUR MONEY'S NEW HOME

Picture this: You've just baked the perfect batch of cookies. They're golden and delicious, and the tantalizing aroma fills the room. Now, where would you store these gems? Have you tossed haphazardly on a table? Of course not! You'd carefully place them in a cookie jar, safe and sound. Think of a bank as that cookie jar, a secure place for your hard-earned dough but with added benefits like interest, convenience, and an array of financial services.

In this chapter, we'll explore the basics of banking, starting with how to choose the right bank for you. It's like choosing the perfect pair of sneakers - you want comfort, style, and a good fit for your needs. So, let's lace up and start this exciting leg of our financial journey!

2.1 CHOOSING THE RIGHT BANK FOR YOU

Factors to Consider When Choosing a Bank

Selecting a bank is crucial and should be based on factors that align with your financial needs and lifestyle. Here are some key considerations:

- **Location and Accessibility:** If you prefer in-person banking, consider a bank with branches and ATMs close to where you live, work, or attend school. Some banks reimburse ATM fees, a handy feature for those on the go.
- **Customer Service:** Top-notch customer service is vital. Look for banks that offer easy access to customer service representatives through phone, email, or online chat.

- **Online and Mobile Banking:** Ensure your bank offers robust online and mobile banking features. This could include mobile check deposits, digital money transfers, and alerts for account activity.
- **Financial Products and Services:** Consider what financial products and services you may need. This could include checking and savings accounts, credit cards, loans, or investment services.
- **Account Fees and Requirements:** Be aware of account fees, minimum balance requirements, or charges for certain transactions. A bank with fewer fees can save you money in the long run.

Traditional Banks vs. Online Banks

Choosing between a traditional bank and an online bank is like choosing between a physical book and an e-book. Both have their advantages, and the best choice depends on your preferences.

Traditional banks have physical branches where you can talk with bank representatives face-to-face. They often offer various services, including checking and savings accounts, loans, and investment services. Many traditional banks also provide online and mobile banking options.

Online banks, on the other hand, operate entirely over the Internet. Without the overhead costs of physical branches, online banks often offer higher interest rates on savings accounts and lower fees. They typically provide 24/7 access to online banking services, and customer service is usually available through phone or online chat.

So, a traditional bank might be your best bet if you prefer face-to-face interactions and a wide range of services. An online bank could be a great fit if you're comfortable banking online and looking for high interest rates and low fees.

The Importance of Checking Fees and Account Requirements

When choosing a bank, reading the fine print about fees and account requirements is essential. It's like checking the nutrition label on your favorite snack. You want to know what you're getting!

Look for information on monthly maintenance fees, ATM fees, overdraft fees, and fees for using other services like money transfers. Some banks waive monthly fees if you maintain a minimum balance or set up direct deposit. Make sure you understand these requirements to avoid unexpected fees.

Also, check the bank's policy on overdrafts. An overdraft occurs when you spend more money than you have in your account. Some banks offer overdraft protection, which covers the overdrawn amount for a fee. Others may decline transactions that would overdraw your account, while some might allow the transaction but charge you an overdraft fee. Understanding these policies can help you avoid unpleasant surprises.

Ultimately, choosing a bank is about finding where your money can grow and where you feel comfortable navigating your financial journey. It's about finding a partner to work with you to achieve your financial goals. So, take your time, research, and choose a bank that fits your needs, like a well-tailored suit or a perfect pair of sneakers. It might seem like a small step, but it's a significant stride towards financial independence.

2.2 TYPES OF BANK ACCOUNTS: CHECKING VS. SAVINGS

So, you've picked out a bank that fits your needs like a glove. Nice work! Now, it's time to understand the types of accounts you'll be handling. Think of it like getting a new phone. You've got the brand and model sorted out; now let's dig into the features, the apps, and the nitty-gritty that makes it all tick. In the banking universe, these features are your checking and savings accounts.

Checking Accounts: Your Everyday Money Manager

Think of a checking account as your assistant for everyday finances. It's an account that allows you to deposit money and then withdraw it for your daily expenses. Your paycheck can be directly deposited into this account, and your bills can be paid from it. It's like the command center for your financial operations!

A checking account is designed for frequent transactions. You can access your money through checks, ATMs, debit cards, and electronic transfers. Imagine having a friend who's always ready to lend you money (without any interest, of course!). That's your checking account for you. It ensures you have quick and easy access to your money whenever needed.

But remember, while checking accounts are fantastic for managing your daily cash flow, there are better options for growing your money.

Savings Accounts: Your Personal Financial Trainer

Enter the savings account - your very own financial fitness coach. Its purpose is to help your money grow over time. Unlike the checking account, which is all about transactions, the savings account is about accumulation.

A savings account offers a safe place to store money you don't need for daily expenses. It's like a piggy bank but better. Why? Because it pays you interest. Yes, you heard it right. When you keep your money in a savings account, the bank pays you for it.

The catch is that savings accounts come with limits on the number of certain types of transactions you can make each month. So, while the checking account is your go-to for everyday transactions, the savings account is where you stash away money for future goals or emergencies.

Interest Rates and Annual Percentage Yield (APY)

Understanding interest rates and annual percentage yield (APY) is like knowing the rules of a game. It's how you strategize and win.

The interest rate is the percentage of your account balance that the bank pays you for keeping your money with them. It's usually quoted as an annual rate. So, if you have $100 in your savings account with an annual interest rate of 1%, you'll earn $1 over a year. It's not a get-rich-quick scheme, but you are earning it!

But wait, there's more. The magic happens when your earnings start earning, too. This is where APY comes into play.

APY considers the effect of compounding, which is when the interest you earn also starts earning interest. It's like a snowball rolling downhill, gathering more snow and growing larger with each roll. The more frequently interest is compounded, the higher the APY and the more money you'll earn.

So, when comparing savings accounts, look at the APY, not just the interest rate. An account with a higher APY will earn you more money over time.

Remember, a checking account is like your day-to-day money manager, handling your transactions and ensuring you have access to your cash when needed. A savings account, on the other hand, is like a personal trainer for your finances, helping your money grow over time.

Understanding the differences between these accounts and how they can work together is vital to managing your money effectively.

And there you have it! With a firm grasp of checking and savings accounts, you're well on your way to becoming a pro at banking basics. But our exploration continues further. Coming up, we'll dive into the virtual world of online banking. Stay tuned!

2.3 NAVIGATING ONLINE BANKING

Picture yourself at a bustling city intersection. There are signs everywhere, people going in every direction, and so much to see and do. Now, imagine this busy intersection is your online banking portal. It may seem chaotic initially, but once you understand the signs and know which direction to go, it becomes a powerful tool for managing your money.

Online Banking: The Safety Dance

First, let's address the elephant in the room — security. In our digital age, where we do everything from ordering pizza to finding a date online, keeping our personal information safe is crucial. The good news is that banks take online security very seriously. They use various measures like encryption, firewalls, and secure logins to protect your information.

But online safety is a two-way street. Here's what you can do to dance safely on the digital banking stage:

- **Passwords:** Create strong, unique passwords for your online banking accounts. And no, "password123" doesn't cut it! Consider using a password manager to help you create and store complex passwords.
- **Public Networks:** Avoid accessing your bank account from public Wi-Fi networks. These networks are only sometimes secure, and hackers could access your information.
- **Phishing:** Be wary of emails or messages asking for your bank details. Your bank will never ask for your password or PIN, so if you receive an email asking for these, it's likely a scam.

Features of Online Banking: Your Personal Finance Toolkit

Just like a Swiss army knife, online banking offers a range of handy tools all in one place. Here's a rundown of some of the key features:

- **Account Management:** View your account balance, recent transactions, and bank statements at a glance. Gone are the days of waiting for your monthly statement to arrive in the mail!
- **Transfers:** Move money between your accounts or send money to others with just a few clicks. Need to split the dinner bill with a friend? Just transfer your share to their account. Easy peasy!

- **Bill Pay:** Set up automatic payments for your regular bills. It's like having a personal assistant who ensures you never miss a payment.
- **Mobile Deposit:** Deposit checks using your smartphone. Just snap a photo of both sides of the check, and the money is deposited into your account (usually a delay of 1-3 days to process before funds are available).

Tracking Your Spending: Your Personal Finance GPS

One of the biggest perks of online banking is the ability to track your spending in real-time. Think of it as a GPS for your money. It can help you understand where your money is going and guide you toward better financial decisions.

Most online banking platforms categorize your spending so you can see how much you spend on groceries, entertainment, bills, and more. Some even offer budgeting tools to help set spending limits in each category.

Regularly reviewing your spending can highlight habits you need to be aware of, like that daily gourmet coffee eating into your savings goal. It can also help you spot any fraudulent transactions quickly. You can immediately alert your bank if you see a transaction you don't recognize.

There you have it! You can quickly and confidently manage your money with a clear understanding of online banking. From the safety measures that protect your information to the handy features that make banking a breeze, you're now ready to navigate the bustling intersection of online banking. Let's keep this momentum going and move on to the next topic: understanding bank statements.

2.4 UNDERSTANDING BANK STATEMENTS

The Story in Your Statement

Think of your bank statement as a monthly newsletter from your money. It tells where your money came from, where it went, and where it's hanging out. It's like your money's diary, documenting its comings and goings, highs and lows.

To read this story, you'll need to understand the different sections of your bank statement. At the top, you'll find your personal information and the statement period - the start and end dates for which the statement applies.

Next comes the account summary, providing a snapshot of your account's activity during the statement period. It starts with your opening balance, the amount in your account at the beginning of the statement period. Then, it lists the total deposits, withdrawals, and fees during the period, followed by your closing balance, which is the amount of money in your account at the end of the statement period.

After the summary, you'll find a detailed list of all transactions during the statement period. Deposits, withdrawals, fees, and interest earned are all there. Each entry typically includes the transaction's date, description, amount, and running balance.

Now that you know how to navigate your bank statement, let's look at some important details to pay attention to.

The Fine Print: Identifying Fees

In banking, not all transactions are about depositing and withdrawing money. Some are about fees. Yes, those pesky charges that can nibble away at your balance like a mouse at a block of cheese.

Fees can pop up in different parts of your bank statement. They might be listed in the account summary, included in the transaction list, or even have their own section. Standard fees include monthly service fees, ATM fees, and overdraft fees.

Not all fees are set in stone. Some, like monthly service fees, can often be waived if you meet specific requirements, like maintaining a minimum balance or setting up direct deposit. If you notice a fee that you need help understanding or think you shouldn't have been charged, feel free to contact your bank. It's your money, and you have a right to know where it's going.

The Importance of Regular Reviews

Just like you wouldn't ignore messages from a friend, don't ignore your bank statement. Regularly reviewing your statement is crucial for several reasons.

First, it can help you track your spending and saving habits. Are you spending more than you thought on eating out? Are you reaching your savings goals? Your bank statement holds the answers.

Second, reviewing your statement can help you spot errors or fraudulent activity. You may have been double-charged for a purchase, or there's a withdrawal you need to remember making. The sooner you spot these issues, the sooner they can be resolved.

Lastly, keeping an eye on your statement can help you avoid fees. You'll be aware of any monthly service fees, and you can spot things that might lead to fees in the future, like a low balance that could lead to an overdraft.

So, make a habit of reviewing your bank statement each month. It's like catching up with a friend. You'll learn what's new, spot problems, and keep the relationship strong.

And there you have it! You've just navigated the nitty-gritty of banking basics. From choosing a bank that suits your needs to understand the role of checking and savings accounts, from taking full advantage of online banking to deciphering your bank statements - you're now equipped with the knowledge to manage your banking like a pro.

Remember, every step you take in understanding these concepts is a stride towards financial independence. You're not just learning about money; you're empowering yourself to make informed decisions and control your financial future. So, take a moment to celebrate your progress. You're doing great, and this is just the beginning! Up next, we'll delve into an exciting world that goes hand in hand with banking - the world of budgeting and saving. Stay tuned!

Ask the Captain

Captain, how do I choose the right bank for my needs?

Arr, young sailor! Choosing a bank is like picking a suitable vessel for a long voyage. Consider what's essential for your journey – whether it's a bank close to your harbor (local branches), one with a sturdy helm (excellent customer service), or maybe a fast ship (online and mobile banking features). Weigh your options and choose the one that'll sail smoothly with your financial goals.

Is there a difference between traditional banks and online banks, Captain?

"Aye, there is! Traditional banks are like classic ships – they have a physical presence and offer a wide range of services. Online banks, however, are like swift schooners, operating over the digital seas. They often offer higher interest rates and lower fees due to their lack of physical branches. Your choice depends on whether ye prefer face-to-face dealings or the convenience of managing your treasure online."

Captain, how can I avoid bank fees that eat into my savings?

"Keep a sharp eye on the horizon, matey! Bank fees can be like hidden reefs, damaging your treasure without you even knowing. Look for banks with low or no monthly fees, understand the requirements to avoid charges, and steer clear of overdrafts. Being aware and proactive is the key to navigating these waters."

What should I use a checking account for, and how is it different from a savings account?

"Your checking account is like your daily supply chest – perfect for frequent transactions, paying bills, and managing day-to-day expenses. On the other hand, savings accounts are like your treasure chests – meant for stowing away gold for future adventures. They offer interest, helping your savings grow, but aren't meant for daily use.

How do I make the most out of online banking, Captain?

"Embrace the modern tools of navigation, young sailor! Online banking can be a treasure map to managing your finances. Use it to check balances, transfer funds, pay bills, and deposit checks with a snap of your magical-looking glass (smartphone). Just ensure you set strong passwords and avoid the stormy seas of public Wi-Fi for safe passage.

Captain, how important is it to review my bank statements?

It's as important as checking the skies before setting sail! Your bank statement tells the tale of your financial journey – where your treasure's been spent, where it's come from, and what remains. Reviewing it helps spot any unexpected leaks (fraudulent transactions) and ensures you're on course with your spending and saving goals.

Finally, Captain, can you advise me on managing my bank accounts effectively?

Chart a course and stick to it! Use your checking account for daily expenses, but avoid letting your treasure sit idle. Regularly transfer some to your savings, where it can grow. Keep an eye on fees and continually review your bank statements. Remember, a good captain is always in command of their ship, just as you should be with your finances!"

The Captain's Guiding Light: Banking Basics
(Key Chapter Takeaways)

1. **Selecting the Right Bank:** Choose a bank that aligns with your lifestyle, considering factors like location, customer service, online and mobile banking features, financial products, and account fees.
2. **Traditional vs. Online Banks:** Traditional banks offer face-to-face interactions and a wide range of

services, while online banks, with no physical branches, often provide higher interest rates and lower fees.

3. **Understanding Account Fees and Requirements:** Pay attention to account fees such as monthly maintenance, ATM, and overdraft fees, and understand the requirements to avoid unexpected charges.

4. **Types of Bank Accounts - Checking and Savings:** Checking accounts are for daily transactions, while savings accounts are designed for accumulating funds with interest over time.

5. **Interest Rates and APY in Savings Accounts:** Learn the difference between interest rates and Annual Percentage Yield (APY), with the latter considering the compound interest effect.

6. **Online Banking Features and Security:** Embrace the convenience of online banking for account management, transfers, bill pay, and mobile deposits, while ensuring strong security practices like robust passwords and awareness of phishing attempts.

7. **Tracking Spending with Online Banking:** Use online banking tools to track and categorize spending, aiding in budgeting and financial management.

8. **Deciphering Bank Statements:** Regularly review bank statements for transaction details, understanding fees, and spotting any errors or fraudulent activities.

9. **Navigating Bank Fees and Charges:** Be aware of various fees detailed in bank statements and understand how to avoid or reduce them.

10. **Building Financial Literacy through Banking:**
    Engage with banking basics to empower yourself,
    making informed decisions and controlling your
    financial future, paving the way for more advanced
    topics like budgeting and saving.

CHAPTER THREE

MONEY MANAGEMENT: MASTERING THE ART OF BUDGETING

I magine you're setting off on a road trip. You have your snacks, your favorite playlist, and a sense of adventure. But wouldn't it be helpful to have a map? A guide that helps you navigate reach your chosen destinations, and even discover some incredible spots along the way. Budgeting is like that map but for your finances. It's a tool that helps you navigate your income and expenses, reach your financial goals, and discover opportunities to save and invest.

So, buckle up! We're about to embark on an exciting trip into the world of budgeting. We'll explore different budgeting methods, the benefits of tracking your income and expenses, and how budgeting can bring you closer to your financial goals. No need to worry about getting lost or running out of fuel. This journey is all about gaining control and confidence in managing your money.

3.1 AN INTRODUCTION TO BUDGETING

The Purpose and Benefits of Budgeting

Think of budgeting as the fitness regime for your finances. Just as a well-rounded fitness regime helps you maintain your health and achieve your fitness goals, a well-planned budget helps maintain your financial health and achieve your financial goals.

The purpose of budgeting is to give every dollar a job. It's about knowing where your money is going and making conscious decisions about how to spend it. But budgeting isn't just about restricting your spending or making you feel guilty about buying that latte. It's about making your money work for you.

The benefits of budgeting are plentiful. It can help you:

- Spot patterns in your spending and identify areas where you can save.
- Plan for future expenses, whether expected ones like rent or unexpected ones like car repairs.
- Save for big goals like a vacation, a new car, or a house.
- Prevent overspending and avoid debt.
- Gain peace of mind knowing that you're in control of your money.

Budgeting is your financial compass, guiding you towards your financial north star.

Different Methods of Budgeting: Finding Your Fit

Just like there's no one-size-fits-all workout, there's no one-size-fits-all budget. Different budgeting methods cater to different needs, habits, and goals. Let's examine two popular strategies: the zero-based budget and the 50/30/20 rule.

Zero-Based Budgeting: The Every Dollar Job

The zero-based budget follows a simple principle: income minus expenses equals zero. In other words, every dollar you earn has a specific job, whether for living expenses, savings, or debt repayment. It's like having a closet where every item of clothing has a designated spot. There's no room for clutter or confusion.

To create a zero-based budget, start by listing all your income for the month. Then, list all your expenses, starting with necessities like rent and groceries, then savings goals, and finally, discretionary spending like entertainment. The objective is to ensure that your income minus your expenses equals zero.

The 50/30/20 Rule: The Balanced Approach

The 50/30/20 rule offers a more flexible approach. It suggests dividing your after-tax income into three categories:

- 50% for needs like rent, groceries, and other bills.
- 30% for wants like dining out, hobbies, or vacations.
- 20% for savings and debt repayment.

It's like a balanced meal, with proportions of proteins, carbs, and fats. You get a bit of everything without overindulging in one category.

These are just two of the many budgeting methods out there. The key is to find a method that fits your lifestyle and financial goals. You can mix and match methods or tweak them to fit your needs. Remember, the best budget is the one you can stick with.

Tracking Income and Expenses: Your Financial Pulse

Tracking your income and expenses is like taking your financial pulse. It gives you a real-time snapshot of your financial health. It's not about obsessing over every penny but understanding your money habits.

Start by listing all your sources of income, including your salary, side gigs, and passive income. This gives you a clear picture of your total income.

Next, list all your expenses. Start with fixed expenses, like rent or mortgage payments, utilities, and subscriptions. Then, move on to variable expenses like groceries, transportation, and entertainment. Remember occasional expenses like gifts, vacations, or car repairs.

The goal is to see where your money is going and whether your spending aligns with your priorities. It's like tracking your food intake while trying to eat healthier. It's not about depriving yourself but about making informed choices that align with your goals.

So, there you have it! You've just taken your first steps into the world of budgeting. You've learned about the purpose and benefits of budgeting, explored different budgeting methods, and understood the importance of tracking your income and expenses. You're well on your way to mastering the art of budgeting. But remember, this is just the beginning. The real magic happens when you put these concepts into practice, and that's what we'll cover in the following sections. So, stay tuned!

3.2 BUDGETING TOOLS AND APPS: YOUR DIGITAL MONEY MANAGERS

We live in a world where there's an app for almost everything. From ordering food to learning a new language, there's a digital tool to assist you. And budgeting is no different. Various apps are available that can turn the task of budgeting from a tedious chore into a breezy, even enjoyable, process.

Popular Budgeting Apps: Meet Your New Best Friends

Let's introduce you to some of the popular budgeting apps that are revolutionizing the way people manage their money:

- **Mint:** This app is like a personal financial advisor that fits in your pocket. Mint allows you to link all your accounts, track your spending, set up budgets, and even get bill reminders. It provides a holistic view of your financial situation at a glance.
- **You Need a Budget (YNAB):** If you're a fan of the zero-based budgeting approach, YNAB is for you. It encourages you to give every dollar a job and adjust your budget as needed throughout the month. YNAB also provides educational resources to help you learn more about managing your money.
- **PocketGuard:** This app is perfect for those wanting to know how much they can safely spend at any moment. PocketGuard factors in your income, bills,

and savings goals to calculate how much disposable income you have left.

- **GoodBudget:** If you're intrigued by the envelope system, GoodBudget digitizes this method for you. You can create digital envelopes for different spending categories and allocate money to each envelope.
- **EveryDollar:** Created by personal finance guru Dave Ramsey, EveryDollar follows the zero-based budgeting approach and syncs with your bank accounts for easy expense tracking.

Making the Most of Your Budgeting App

Much like learning to ride a bike, using a budgeting app effectively takes some practice. Here are some tips to help you become a budgeting app whizz:

- **Link Your Accounts:** Most budgeting apps can link your bank and credit card accounts. Doing so lets you have all your financial information in one place, and the app can track your income and expenses automatically.
- **Set Up Your Budget:** Spend time setting up your budget in the app. Add your income, fixed expenses, and variable expenses. Define your savings goals and allocate money for entertainment and other discretionary spending.
- **Regularly Review Your Budget:** Make a habit of checking your budgeting app regularly. See where your money is going, whether you're sticking to your

budget, and identify any areas where you could cut back.

- **Use the App's Features:** Explore all the features your budgeting app offers. This could include bill reminders, savings goals trackers, credit score updates, etc.
- **Adjust Your Budget as Needed:** Your budget is never set in stone. Adjust your budget if you need to spend more in one category and underspend in another consistently. The goal is to create a budget that works for you and your lifestyle.

Privacy and Security: Protecting Your Financial Information

While budgeting apps offer convenience and ease, it's essential to be mindful of privacy and security. After all, you're entrusting these apps with sensitive financial information. Here are some precautions to consider:

- **Please read the Privacy Policy:** Before using a budgeting app, read its privacy policy. The Privacy Policy will tell you what information the app collects, how it uses your data, and who it shares it with.
- **Check Security Measures:** Look for budgeting apps with encryption to protect your data. Also, check if the app has measures to protect your account, like two-factor authentication.
- **Use Strong Passwords:** Create a robust and unique password for your budgeting app. Consider

using a password manager to help you generate and
store secure passwords.

- **Monitor Your Accounts:** Regularly check your
linked accounts for any suspicious activity. Contact
your bank or credit card company immediately if you
notice anything unusual.

Embracing budgeting apps can make managing your money
easier and more efficient. By choosing the right app, using it
effectively, and taking steps to protect your financial information, you're leveraging technology to take charge of your financial future. Remember, budgeting isn't about restricting
yourself – it's about understanding your money and empowering yourself to make intelligent financial decisions. You're
not just creating a budget; you're creating a brighter financial
future. So, here's to you and your success in mastering the art
of budgeting!

3.3 THE ENVELOPE SYSTEM: A TRIED AND TRUE METHOD

The Envelope System in Action

Let's picture ourselves in a kitchen, the heart of a household,
where ingredients are transformed into delicious meals. The
envelope system works similarly, transforming your income
into a well-planned budget.

In essence, the envelope system involves dividing your income
into various "envelopes," each representing a different category
of your budget. These could include groceries, rent, utilities,

transportation, entertainment, etc. The idea is to set aside a specific amount of cash in each envelope for the month. Once an envelope is empty, that's it - no more spending in that category until the next month.

This method can be implemented using actual envelopes and cash or, figuratively, multiple bank accounts or budgeting apps. It's like sorting ingredients into different bowls before cooking - it keeps things organized and prevents you from overusing or running out of an ingredient.

Advantages of the Envelope System

Like a reliable recipe, the envelope system has several benefits that make your budgeting process smoother and more effective.

- **Simplicity:** The envelope system is straightforward to understand. There are no complicated calculations or fancy financial jargon. It's as simple as sorting your money into different envelopes and spending only what's in each envelope.
- **Control:** The envelope system gives you a clear view of how much money you have left in each category at any given time. It's like having a measuring cup for each ingredient - you know exactly how much you have left.
- **Accountability:** With the envelope system, there's no room for overspending. Once an envelope is empty, you stop spending in that category. It's a built-

in accountability system that encourages responsible spending.

- **Flexibility:** The envelope system is easily adjustable. If you've allocated too much or too little to a category, you can adjust the amounts in your envelopes for the next month. It's like tweaking a recipe to suit your taste.

Success with the Envelope System: Your Recipe for a Healthy Budget

Just as each kitchen has its unique rhythm, the envelope system requires fine-tuning to work effectively. Here are some tips to help you succeed with this budgeting method:

- **Start with a Plan:** Before filling envelopes with cash, sit down and plan your budget. Determine how much money you need in each category based on your income and expenses. It's like planning a menu before you start cooking.
- **Use Cash for Tangible Categories:** The envelope system works best for categories where you can pay with cash, like groceries, dining out and entertainment. For expenses like rent or utilities, where you might pay electronically, consider a virtual envelope system using a budgeting app or multiple bank accounts.
- **Regularly Review and Adjust:** Getting your envelope amounts right may take a few months. Periodically review your spending and adjust your

envelopes as needed. Remember, the goal is to create a budget that works for you.

- **Be Consistent:** The envelope system is not a one-off thing. It requires consistent practice. But over time, it can become a habit that helps you manage your money effectively.

You can transform your income into a well-planned, effective budget using the envelope system. It's like mastering a favorite recipe - it might take some practice, but the results are worth it. So, roll up your sleeves, grab your envelopes, and let's get budgeting!

3.4 TAILORING YOUR BUDGET TO YOUR GOALS

Setting Short-Term and Long-Term Financial Goals

Every great endeavor begins with a goal, a target to aim for. In finance, these targets are short-term and long-term financial goals.

Short-term goals are like pit stops on a road trip, achievable within a year or less. This could be anything from saving for a new smartphone, paying off a small debt, or even setting aside money for holiday gifts. These goals keep you motivated and help you see the progress you're making on your financial journey.

Long-term goals, however, are like the ultimate destination of your road trip, achievable in more than a year. This could include saving for a down payment on a house, planning a dream vacation, or building a retirement nest egg. These goals might seem far off, but every step you take brings you closer.

When setting these goals, make them SMART - Specific, Measurable, Achievable, Relevant, and Time-bound. Instead of "I want to save money," make your goal "I want to save $3000 for a down payment on a car in the next 18 months." A SMART goal gives you a clear target to aim for and makes it easier to track your progress.

Adjusting Your Budget to Meet Your Goals

Think of your budget as a financial workout routine. Just as you might adjust your workout to achieve your fitness goals, you'll need to adjust your budget to achieve your financial goals.

Start by looking at your current budget. Are there areas where you could cut back? You could eat out less often or downgrade your phone plan. These savings might seem small, but they add up over time, and every dollar saved brings you closer to your goal.

Next, look at your income. Could you increase it? You could take on a part-time job, sell unused items, or turn a hobby into a side hustle. Think outside the box and explore ways to boost your income.

Adjust your budget once you've identified ways to save and earn more. Allocate the extra money towards your financial goals. It's like adding extra push-ups to your workout to build your strength faster.

Regularly Reviewing and Adjusting Your Budget

A budget isn't a set-it-and-forget-it kind of deal. It's more like a garden that needs regular tending. Regularly reviewing your budget allows you to see if you're on track to meet your goals, identify areas for improvement, and adjust as needed.

Set a time each month to review your budget. Look at your spending in each category. Did you stay within your budget? If not, why not? Were there unexpected expenses? Can you plan for them in the future? Use this time to reflect on your spending habits and identify ways to improve.

Also, review your financial goals. Are you making progress towards them? If not, what's holding you back? Do you need to adjust your goals or your budget? Remember, it's okay to make changes. Your budget should be flexible, adapting to your needs and circumstances.

With your goals set, budget adjusted, and a commitment to regular reviews, you're well on your way to mastering money management. Remember, budgeting isn't about restriction; it's about making conscious decisions on how to spend your money. It's about guiding your money to where it can best serve you. So, here's to you and your financial fitness journey. You're doing a fantastic job; the best is yet to come! Next, we will explore an important aspect of financial health: saving. So, let's keep the momentum going and continue on this exciting path towards financial confidence and success.

Ask the Captain

Captain, why is budgeting so important? I just want to enjoy my money now!

Ahoy, young sailor! Budgeting is like charting a course before a sea voyage. It's not about restricting how much treasure you can spend but about ensuring you have enough for smooth sailing and stormy weather. By budgeting, you ensure you can enjoy your money now and save some for future adventures!

How do I choose a budgeting method that works for me, Captain?

Choosing a budgeting method is like picking the correct ship for your journey. Some prefer the strict guidelines of a zero-based budget, like a sturdy ship, giving every dollar a job. Others might favor the flexibility of the 50/30/20 rule, akin to an elegant sloop. The key is to try different methods and see which suits your financial seas best!"

Captain, how can I track my spending effectively? It seems overwhelming.

Tracking your spending is like keeping a log on a long voyage. Start simple. Keep a record of your income and expenses. You can use budgeting apps, like having a first mate who monitors your finances. Over time, you'll see patterns in your spending, helping you navigate your financial waters more wisely.

Are budgeting apps safe to use, Captain? I'm worried about my financial info.

Budgeting apps can be as safe as a well-guarded treasure chest, matey! Just make sure you choose apps with sturdy locks – look for encryption and robust security features. Use unique pass-words and be cautious about the networks you use to access your accounts. Remember, the safety of your treasure is partly in your hands!

What's this 'envelope system' I've heard about, Captain? Does it really work?

The envelope system is a classic, like an old map guiding you to buried treasure. You divide your money into envelopes,' each for a specific category like provisions or repairs. Once the envelope is empty, no more spending in that category. It's a tangible way to keep your budget on course!

How do I adjust my budget for my goals, Captain?

Adjusting your budget for goals is like setting sails for a distant shore. First, identify your short-term and long-term goals and your financial destinations. Then, adjust your spending and savings to ensure you're headed in the right direction. Cutting back on some expenses or finding ways to boost your income will give you budget flexibility.

Captain, how often should I review my budget?

Reviewing your budget should be as regular as checking the stars for navigation. Do it monthly to ensure you're on track. Look at your spending in each category and adjust as needed. Remember, a budget is a living document, changing as the tides. Regular reviews keep you sailing smoothly towards your financial goals!

The Captain's Guiding Light: Money Management (Key Chapter Takeaways)

1. **Budgeting as a Financial Navigation Tool:** Budgeting is crucial for managing your income and expenses, helping you reach financial goals and find opportunities to save and invest.
2. **Understanding the Purpose of Budgeting:** Budgeting allows for a clear understanding of spending patterns, planning for future expenses,

achieving savings goals, avoiding debt, and gaining control over financial decisions.

3. **Different Budgeting Methods:** Explore methods like zero-based budgeting (every dollar has a job) and the 50/30/20 rule (allocating income to needs, wants, and savings/debt repayment) to find what best suits your financial habits and goals.

4. **Importance of Tracking Income and Expenses:** Regularly tracking all sources of income and expenses is vital for a clear financial picture and making informed spending choices.

5. **Utilizing Budgeting Tools and Apps:** Leverage technology with apps like Mint, YNAB, PocketGuard, GoodBudget, and EveryDollar to simplify budgeting, track spending, set budgets, and manage accounts effectively.

6. **The Envelope System for Budget Management:** This method involves dividing income into categories and using physical or digital 'envelopes' to limit spending in each category, fostering discipline and control.

7. **Advantages of the Envelope System:** Provides simplicity, clear control over spending, accountability, and flexibility in budgeting.

8. **Setting and Adjusting Budgets to Financial Goals:** Align your budget with short-term and long-term financial goals, making it specific, measurable, achievable, relevant, and time-bound (SMART).

9. **Regular Budget Reviews and Adjustments:** Conduct monthly budget reviews to track progress,

identify areas for improvement, and make necessary adjustments to stay aligned with financial goals.

10. **Empowerment Through Budgeting Mastery:** Understanding and effectively implementing budgeting strategies empowers individuals to make intelligent financial decisions, leading to improved financial health and goal achievement.

CHAPTER FOUR

SAVINGS - IT'S NOT JUST FOR GROWN-UPS

Picture this. You're at the starting line of a marathon, surrounded by runners of all ages. Among them is a group of young teenagers, lacing up their shoes and warming up enthusiastically. Some spectators might wonder, aren't they too young to run a marathon? But, as the race begins and these young runners pace themselves steadily, it becomes clear — starting early gives them a unique advantage. They have time on their side.

The same principle applies to saving money. Starting early can put you ahead of the game, giving you a decisive advantage — time. In this chapter, we'll explore the benefits of starting to save at a young age, the magic of compound interest, and how to set and reach your savings goals.

4.1 THE POWER OF STARTING EARLY

The Early Bird Gets the Interest

Starting to save at a young age has several benefits. First, it helps build the habit of saving. Just like learning to play an instrument or mastering a new sport, the earlier you start, the more ingrained the habit becomes.

Second, starting to save in your teens gives your money more time to grow. This is where a magical concept known as compound interest comes into play.

The Magic of Compound Interest: Your Money's Personal Trainer

Imagine your savings as a runner. With every lap around the track (or year), the runner gains strength and speed (interest).

What if the runners could clone themselves at the end of each lap, adding another runner to the race? That's what compound interest does to your money.

Here's how it works: You start by earning interest on your saved money. Then, you earn interest on that interest. And then you earn interest on that interest. And so on. It's like your money's personal trainer, helping it grow stronger financially the more you work at it.

Setting Savings Goals: Your Financial Roadmap

Knowing the benefits of saving early and the power of compound interest is excellent. But how do you get started?

Begin by setting savings goals. These are specific targets that you want to reach with your savings. For example, your short-term goal could be to save $500 for a new laptop. A long-term goal might be to save $20,000 for a down payment on a house.

Setting savings goals gives you a clear target to aim for and makes saving feel more purposeful. It's like having a roadmap for your marathon, showing you where you're going and how far you've come.

Next, make a plan. Decide how much money you'll set aside from each paycheck towards your savings goals. Be realistic about what you can afford to save. Even if it's a small amount, remember that every dollar counts and can grow over time thanks to compound interest.

Finally, stick to your plan. Consistency is vital when it comes to saving. It might be challenging, but remember the benefits of starting early and the power of compound interest. You're not just saving money but building a solid foundation for your financial future.

So, lace up your shoes and get ready to run your savings marathon. With the power of starting early, the magic of compound interest, and a clear savings plan, you're prepared to take on the race. Remember, it's not about how fast you go; it's about pacing yourself and keeping your eye on the finish line. You've got this!

4.2 SETTING REALISTIC SAVING GOALS

SMART Savings Goals: Your Financial Blueprint

Imagine you're building a treehouse. Before hammering away, you'll need a blueprint - a detailed plan that guides your construction and helps you visualize the final product. In finance, SMART goals serve as your blueprint, providing a clear and detailed plan for your savings.

SMART is an acronym for Specific, Measurable, Achievable, Relevant, and Time-bound. Let's break down what these terms mean when setting savings goals.

- **Specific:** Your goal should be clear and well-defined. Instead of "I want to save money," aim for something more specific, like "I want to save $2000 for a used car."

- **Measurable:** Your goal should be quantifiable. It should include a specific amount you want to save, allowing you to track your progress and know when you've achieved your goal.
- **Achievable:** Your goal should be realistic and attainable. It should stretch your abilities but remain possible. If you're saving $50 a month, a goal to save $5000 in three months might not be achievable.
- **Relevant:** Your goal should align with your broader financial plan and personal aspirations. If your long-term goal is to buy a house, a short-term goal might be to save for a down payment.
- **Time-bound:** Your goal should have a deadline. A deadline creates a sense of urgency and can motivate you to stay on track. Instead of "I want to save $2000," aim for "I want to save $2000 in 12 months."

Setting SMART goals creates a clear, detailed, and practical blueprint for your savings. You're not just dreaming about a treehouse but planning how to build it.

Balancing Goals with Spending Needs: The Financial Tightrope

Now, setting savings goals is a crucial part of money management. But it's equally important to balance these goals with your spending needs. Managing your finances can feel like walking a tightrope, with savings on one side and spending on the other.

On the spending side, you have your living expenses, such as rent, groceries, transportation, and utilities. You may also have discretionary spending, like dining out, entertainment, and hobbies.

On the savings side, you have your short-term and long-term goals. These could range from saving for a vacation or a new laptop to setting aside money for retirement or a down payment on a home.

The key is to find a balance between these two sides. You want to save enough to reach your goals while meeting your daily needs and enjoying your life. This balance will look different for everyone, and finding what works best for you might take time and adjustments.

Celebrating Milestones: The Savers' Victory Lap

Setting savings goals and working towards them can sometimes feel like a marathon. And just like in a marathon, it's important to celebrate your milestones along the way.

Did you reach a quarter of your savings goal? Celebrate it! Did you manage to save consistently for six months? That's a victory! Did you resist an impulse buy and put that money into savings instead? Pat yourself on the back!

Celebrating your milestones, big and small, can motivate you to keep going. It can make saving more enjoyable and reinforce the habit of saving.

Remember, saving money isn't about depriving yourself. It's a positive, empowering choice that you're making for your future self. So, don't be shy about celebrating your progress. Each milestone is a testament to your commitment, discipline, and financial savvy.

There you have it! You've just explored how to set SMART savings goals, balance these goals with your spending needs, and celebrate your savings milestones. With these strategies in your financial toolkit, you're ready to build your savings and work towards your financial goals with confidence and clarity.

4.3 CREATIVE WAYS TO SAVE ON A TIGHT BUDGET

Pinching Pennies: Everyday Savings Tips

Imagine you're on a treasure hunt, but instead of searching for gold, you're searching for savings. The great news is that potential savings are hiding in your everyday expenses, waiting to be discovered. Let's look at some strategies to unearth these hidden treasures.

- **Do-it-yourself:** Whether brewing your coffee, packing your lunch, or mending your clothes, doing things yourself can save you a surprising amount of money. Plus, it can be fun and satisfying!

- **Second-hand Savings:** Before you rush to buy something new, consider if you can buy it second-hand, borrow it, or even swap for it. Thrift stores, online marketplaces, and changing groups can be gold mines for savings.
- **Cost-cutting Subscriptions:** Review your subscriptions regularly. Do you need all those streaming services? Can you switch to a cheaper phone plan? Small changes can add up to significant savings over time.
- **Smart Shopping:** Plan your meals around sales, buy in bulk, and don't shop when hungry. These simple strategies can shave a significant amount off your grocery bill.

Fun with Finances: Savings Challenges and Games

Saving money doesn't have to be a chore. It can be downright fun when you incorporate challenges and games. Here's how you can add excitement to your savings routine.

- **Penny-a-Day Challenge:** Start by saving one penny on day one, two pennies on day two, and so on. By the end of the year, you'll have saved $667.95!
- **Round-Up Game:** Every time you purchase, round up the amount and transfer the difference into savings. Many banks and budgeting apps offer this feature.

- **Spend Nothing Days:** Challenge yourself to have a certain number of days each month where you don't spend any money.
- **52-Week Savings Challenge:** Save $1 in week one, $2 in week two, and so on. By the end of 52 weeks, you'll have saved $1,378!

Boost Your Budget: The Power of Side Hustles

Imagine boosting your income by doing something you love or are good at. Welcome to the world of side hustles, where your passion, skills, and spare time can translate into extra cash.

- **Freelancing:** Do you like graphic design, writing, or social media? Platforms like Upwork and Fiverr connect freelancers with clients who need their skills.
- **Sell Handmade Goods:** If you love crafting, consider selling your creations on Etsy or at local craft fairs.
- **Tutoring:** If you excel in a particular subject, consider offering tutoring services in your spare time.
- **Pet Sitting or Dog Walking:** If you love animals, pet sitting or dog walking can be a great way to earn extra cash.

Remember, every little bit helps when saving on a tight budget. By finding creative ways to save, making saving fun, and boosting your income with side hustles, you're stretching your dollars and shaping your financial future. So, put on your treasure hunter hat and start discovering the potential savings in your everyday life. You're well on your way to building a savings stash for which your future self will thank you.

4.4 THE MAGIC OF COMPOUND INTEREST

Have you ever watched a snowball rolling down a hill? It starts small, but as it rolls, it picks up more snow and grows bigger. By the time it reaches the bottom, it's a giant, impressive snowball. Now, imagine your savings as that small snowball. As it rolls down the hill of time, it doesn't just pick up more snow (or money); it also picks up speed, growing faster and faster. That, my friends, is the magic of compound interest.

Understanding How Compound Interest Works: The Snowball Effect

Compound interest works by earning interest not just on your initial savings (the principal) but also on the interest your savings already earned. It's interest on interest, or as I like to call it, the "snowball effect."

Let's say you have $100 in a savings account that earns an annual interest rate of 5%. After one year, you'll earn $5 in interest, bringing your total to $105. Now, here's where the magic happens. In the second year, you'll earn interest not just on your original $100 but also on the $5 in interest you've earned. So, you'll earn $5.25 in interest, bringing your total to $110.25. This might not seem like a big difference, but as time goes on, this effect becomes more and more powerful.

Seeing Compound Interest in Action: Meet Your New Best Friend, The Savings Calculator

Visualizing compound interest can be tricky, especially when dealing with more significant amounts and longer periods. Luckily, a handy tool can help – a savings calculator.

A savings calculator lets you see how your money could grow over time with compound interest. You just input your starting balance, monthly deposit, interest rate, and the years you plan to save, and the calculator does the rest. It's like a crystal ball showing you your potential financial future.

Let's say you're 16 and start saving $50 a month in a savings account that earns an annual interest rate of 3%. By the time you're 26, you'll have saved $6,000. But thanks to compound interest, your balance will be over $7,000!

The Impact of Compound Interest Over Time: Your Secret Weapon for Financial Success

The power of compound interest lies in its potential to grow your savings exponentially over time. The longer your money stays in the account, the more interest it earns and the faster it grows. It's like that snowball rolling down the hill, picking up speed as it gets bigger.

This is why starting to save early is so powerful. The earlier you start, the more time your money has to grow. Keep going even if you can only save a small amount each month.

Remember, with compound interest, every dollar you save is a seed that can grow into a money tree over time.

So there you have it! You've unlocked the magic of compound interest and learned how it can be your secret weapon for financial success. With this powerful tool in your arsenal, you're saving money and setting the stage for your money to grow and flourish. It's like planting a garden – with time, patience, and the magic of compound interest, and you're cultivating a rich and bountiful financial future.

As we wrap up this chapter, take a moment to reflect on the insights you've gained. From understanding the power of starting early to setting SMART savings goals, from finding creative ways to save to harnessing the magic of compound interest, you've taken significant steps towards building a solid savings strategy.

Like a marathon runner, remember to pace yourself, celebrate your milestones, and watch the finish line. After all, the journey to financial independence isn't a sprint; it's a marathon. And every step you take, no matter how small, brings you closer to your financial goals. So keep going, keep growing, and watch as your savings snowball roll bigger and faster. You're doing a fantastic job; your future self will thank you.

And now, as we turn the page, we'll delve into a topic that often feels like a mystery to many – understanding credit. It's a journey that will take us from the basics of credit scores to the ins and outs of credit cards. So, get ready because this next chapter will be an enlightening adventure!

Ask the Captain

Captain, why is it so important to start saving early? Can't I just start when I'm older?

Ahoy, young mate! Starting to save early is like catching the wind in your sails right from the harbor. The earlier you start, the more time your money has to grow through the magic of compound interest. It's like planting a seedling early so you can enjoy a sturdy tree sooner rather than later.

What exactly is compound interest, Captain? It doesn't sound very easy.

Imagine compound interest as a trusty crew that keeps working even while you sleep. You start with your savings, then earn interest on it. Next year, you earn interest not just on your original savings but also on the interest you earned before. Over time, this snowballs, growing your treasure faster than just stashing it in a chest!

How do I set realistic savings goals, Captain? I don't want to aim too high or too low.

Setting sail without a destination can leave you adrift. For savings, use the SMART method: Specific, Measurable, Achievable, Relevant, and Time-bound goals. It's like charting a course that's challenging but possible. Set clear targets, like saving for a new spyglass, and give yourself a timeline to achieve it.

Captain, I'm on a tight budget. How can I save without feeling like I'm sacrificing everything?

Even the tiniest leak can sink a great ship; similarly, small savings add up. Look for little ways to cut back, like making meals at home instead of always dining at port. Also, consider a side hustle – it's like finding new trade routes for extra gold. Every coin saved is a step towards your treasure chest.

Can you explain more about how to use a savings calculator, Captain?

A savings calculator is like a navigator for your treasure. Input your starting amount, how much you'll add to your monthly savings, the interest rate, and how long you plan to save. It'll chart your course, showing how much your savings will grow. It helps visualize the distant shores you're aiming for.

Captain, isn't staying motivated while saving for long-term goals hard?

Staying the course requires patience, just like a long sea voyage. Celebrate your milestones – hitting the quarter-mark of your goal or saving consistently for six months. These victories are like favorable winds pushing your ship closer to its destination. Remember, every bit saved is progress!

Finally, Captain, any last words of advice for young savers like me?

Always keep an eye on the horizon! Start saving early, be consistent, and remember the power of compound interest. Your future is like uncharted waters, and saving is your compass. You'll reach the shores you once only dreamed of with time and patience. So, set your sails and let the voyage begin!

The Captain's Guiding Light: Savings (Key Chapter Takeaways)

1. **Starting Early with Savings:** Begin saving at a young age to build a habit, allowing more time for your money to grow through compound interest.
2. **Understanding Compound Interest:** Compound interest, akin to a snowball effect, helps your savings grow exponentially over time as you earn interest on your principal and accumulated interest.
3. **Setting SMART Savings Goals:** Create specific, measurable, achievable, relevant, and time-bound (SMART) savings goals to provide a clear and practical blueprint for your financial savings journey.

4. **Balancing Savings with Spending:** Find a balance between saving for the future and meeting current spending needs, ensuring a sustainable and enjoyable financial lifestyle.

5. **Celebrating Financial Milestones:** Acknowledge and celebrate milestones in your savings journey, fostering motivation and positive reinforcement for your financial habits.

6. **Implementing Creative Savings Strategies:** Employ creative ways to save money, even on a tight budget, through DIY activities, smart shopping, and utilizing second-hand options.

7. **Incorporating Fun into Saving:** Engage in savings challenges and games to make the process enjoyable and maintain enthusiasm in your financial journey.

8. **Exploring Side Hustles for Extra Income:** Boost your savings potential by engaging in side hustles or freelance opportunities that align with your skills and interests.

9. **Maximizing the Potential of Compound Interest:** Utilize savings calculators to visualize and maximize the impact of compound interest over time, emphasizing the power of early and consistent savings.

10. **Developing a Robust Savings Strategy:** Combine the principles of early saving, SMART goal setting, creative saving techniques, and the magic of compound interest to develop a strong and effective

savings strategy, setting a foundation for long-term
financial success and stability.

CHAPTER FIVE

NAVIGATING THE CREDIT CARD MAZE

P ull a card from a deck. What do you see? It could be an ace, a joker, or a queen, all of which mean something different for a card game. Now, imagine pulling a credit card from your wallet. It might not determine the outcome of a game, but it sure can shape your financial life.

Credit cards - they're small, shiny, and convenient. But behind that little piece of plastic lies a world of possibilities, responsibilities, and potential pitfalls. This chapter will explore this world and unravel the intricacies of credit cards. Let's start with the basics.

5.1 UNDERSTANDING CREDIT CARDS: THE GOOD, THE BAD, AND THE UGLY

Credit Card Basics: The Financial Swiss Army Knife

A credit card is a versatile financial tool. Think of it as a Swiss army knife in your financial toolkit. It allows you to borrow up to a specific limit to make purchases or withdraw cash. At the end of each billing cycle, you either pay the balance in full, make a minimum payment, or pay an amount somewhere between.

It's like having a mini loan in your pocket, ready to use whenever needed. But like any tool, it's essential to use it responsibly and understand how it works to prevent potential harm.

Interest Rates and Fees: The Price Tag of Convenience

The convenience of a credit card comes with a price tag – interest rates and fees. Interest, also known as Annual Percentage Rate (APR), is the cost of borrowing money. If you don't pay your balance in full each month, you will be charged interest on the remaining balance. It's like renting a movie - if you don't return it on time, you pay extra.

Fees are another part of a credit card's price tag. These can include annual, late payment, and cash advance fees, among others. Reading the fine print in your credit card agreement is crucial to understand all potential fees.

Rewards and Perks: The Sunny Side of Credit Cards

Credit cards aren't all about fees and interest. On the sunny side, they offer rewards and perks that can make them attractive financial tools.

Rewards can come in many forms, such as cashback, travel miles, or points that can be redeemed for goods, services, or experiences. It's like getting a little bonus every time you use your card.

Perks are the extra benefits that come with a credit card. These can include travel insurance, extended warranties, and access to exclusive events. It's like having a VIP pass in your pocket.

Potential Risks and Downsides: Navigating the Credit Card Maze

While credit cards offer convenience, rewards, and perks, they have potential downsides and risks. One of the primary risks is the temptation to overspend. With a credit limit that may be higher than your monthly income, it's easy to fall into the trap of buying now and worrying about paying later.

Credit card debt can spiral quickly due to high interest rates and minimum payments barely covering the interest. It's like trying to fill up a leaky bucket - more trickles out as you pour money in.

Another risk is the potential damage to your credit score if you fail to make timely payments. Your credit score is like your financial reputation, affecting your ability to get loans, rent apartments, and sometimes even get jobs.

Credit cards can lead to identity theft if your card information falls into the wrong hands. It's like dropping your house key - if someone unscrupulous finds it, they can access your home.

Understanding the basics of credit cards, including the convenience they offer, the costs associated with them, the rewards and perks they can provide, and the potential downsides and risks, is the first step towards using them wisely. It's like learning the rules of a new game - once you understand them, you can play strategically and win. So, let's move on to the next part of the game - learning how to use a credit card wisely.

5.2 HOW TO USE A CREDIT CARD WISELY

Paying Balances in Full: The Financial Full Stop

Think of your credit card balance as a story. Each purchase you make adds a new sentence to the tale. By the end of the month, you've written an entire chapter. But you don't want this story to continue into the next month. Paying your credit card balance in full each month is like putting a complete stop at the end of the chapter in a novel.

Why is this important? Paying off your balance in full means you won't be charged interest on your purchases. It's like shopping at a sale - you get what you need without paying the total price. It also signals to credit bureaus that you're responsible with credit, which can help boost your credit score.

Utilizing Credit Limit Responsibly: The Financial High Jump

Your credit limit is the maximum amount you can charge to your credit card. It's like the bar in a high jump competition. Just because you can jump that high doesn't mean you should every time. Regularly maxing out your credit card can signal to lenders that you're a high-risk borrower.

A good rule of thumb is to keep your credit utilization - the ratio of your credit card balance to your credit limit - under 30%. If your credit limit is $1000, keep your balance under

$300. It's like warming up before a high jump - it prepares you for the leap without straining your muscles.

Avoiding Late Payments: The Financial Timekeeper

Making your credit card payment on time might seem like a no-brainer, but life can sometimes throw us off track. However, late payments can result in fees, increased interest rates, and negative marks on your credit report. It's like showing up late for a game - you might miss an essential play and let your team down.

To avoid late payments, set up automatic payments or a reminder to make your payment a few days before it's due. It's like setting an alarm before a game - it ensures you show up on time, ready to play.

Maximizing Rewards and Cash Back: The Financial Bonus Round

If your credit card offers rewards or cash back, take full advantage of these benefits. It's like playing a bonus round in a game - it allows you to earn extra points.

Understand how your rewards program works. Do you earn more points for certain types of purchases? Are there any special promotions or bonuses you can qualify for? It's like studying the game's rules - it helps you strategize and score the most points.

Rewards and cashback can offer significant benefits, but they shouldn't encourage you to overspend. Always stick to your budget and pay your balance in full each month. It's like playing the game wisely - you aim to win, but not at the cost of your well-being.

So, there you have it. You're now equipped with strategies to use your credit card wisely. From paying your balance in full each month to keeping your credit utilization low, from avoiding late payments to maximizing rewards, these practices can help you confidently navigate the credit card maze. It's like mastering the rules of a new game - once you know how to play, you can play to win. But remember, the game of credit isn't just about winning - it's about playing responsibly, knowing when to pass, and when to score. With these strategies in your playbook, you're all set to make wise credit decisions today and in the future. Let the game begin!

5.3 THE IMPACTS OF CREDIT CARD DEBT

Impact on Credit Score: The Financial Report Card

Let's start with your credit score, which is like your financial report card. This three-digit number tells lenders how likely you are to repay borrowed money. A high score can open doors to loans, new credit cards, and even better interest rates. But a low score? It can slam those doors shut.

Whenever you miss a credit card payment, it's like forgetting to submit an assignment. It negatively impacts your credit score, just like a missed assignment affects your class grade. And with each passing month, the damage gets worse. It's like getting a red mark on your report card that everyone can see.

Credit bureaus, the entities that calculate your credit score, consider payment history a significant factor. So, having credit card debt and missing payments can seriously harm your credit score. It's like being stuck at the bottom of your class rankings. But in this case, it's a ranking that follows you every time you want to borrow money.

Financial Stress and Anxiety: The Emotional Toll

While credit card debt's impact on your credit score is quantifiable, the emotional toll is more challenging but just as significant. Dealing with debt can lead to financial stress and anxiety. It's like having a dark cloud hanging over your head, casting a shadow on your daily life.

You might lose sleep worrying about how to make your next payment. Knowing you're adding to your debt, you might feel anxious every time you use your credit card. It's like being unable to enjoy a sunny day because you constantly worry about the next storm.

This stress and anxiety can also spill over into other aspects of your life. It can affect your performance at school, your relationships, and even your physical health. It's like carrying a heavy backpack everywhere you go. It weighs you down and makes even simple tasks feel difficult.

Long-Term Financial Consequences: The Domino Effect

Credit card debt can also lead to long-term financial consequences. It's like knocking over a domino and watching the rest topple one by one.

For starters, the high interest rates on credit card debt mean you'll pay much more than you initially borrowed. It's like buying a candy bar and ending up with a bill for a gourmet meal.

This debt can also make saving money or investing in the future challenging. It's like trying to fill a bucket with a hole in the bottom. No matter how much you pour in, you never get ahead.

And remember that damaged credit score? It can make getting loans for big purchases like a car or a house harder. Even if you get approved, you'll likely face higher interest rates because of your lower credit score. It's like having to climb a mountain while everyone else gets to take the elevator.

Debt Collection Practices: The Unwanted Visitors

If you fail to make credit card payments, your debt may be turned over to a collection agency. These agencies use tactics to get you to pay, from constant phone calls to threatening letters. It's like having a swarm of bees following you around, buzzing in your ear.

Dealing with debt collectors can be stressful and intimidating, so knowing your rights is essential. The Fair Debt Collection Practices Act protects against abusive, unfair, or deceptive collection practices. It's like having a shield to defend yourself against those buzzing bees.

So, there you have it. The impacts of credit card debt reach far beyond your wallet. They can affect your credit score, emotional well-being, long-term financial stability, and even personal peace. It's a maze with many twists and turns. But the good news is that you can avoid getting lost in this maze with knowledge and careful navigation. You can use credit cards to build your credit and enhance your financial life rather than letting them drag you into debt.

5.4 BUILDING GOOD CREDIT EARLY

Importance of On-Time Payments: The Timekeeper of Credit

Imagine you're a basketball player, and the final seconds of a crucial game are ticking away. Every pass, every dribble, and every shot matters. In the world of credit, on-time payments are those critical shots. Paying your credit card bill on time, every time, is one of the most effective ways to build good credit.

Each timely payment you make adds a positive mark to your credit history, like scoring points in a game. On the other hand, late or missed payments are like missed shots, negatively impacting your score. Payment history makes up a significant portion of your credit score. So, consider setting up automatic payments or reminders to ensure you never miss your due date. It's like having a coach constantly reminding you of the game strategy.

Keeping Credit Utilization Low: The Balancing Act of Credit

Now, let's move on to credit utilization, which refers to the proportion of your available credit that you're using. It's like a balancing act in a circus. On one side of the rope, you have your credit limit, the total amount of credit available. Conversely, you have your balance, the amount you owe.

Keeping your credit utilization low means maintaining a balance between these two sides. As a rule of thumb, keeping your utilization below 30% is wise. So, if your credit limit is $1000, try not to carry a balance of more than $300. This shows lenders that you're responsible with your credit and can manage it wisely. It's like a circus performer maintaining perfect balance on the tightrope, demonstrating skill and control.

Length of Credit History: The Marathon of Credit

Think of the length of your credit history as a marathon. It's a long race, and every step counts. Your credit history starts from the moment you open your first credit account, and it includes the ages of your oldest and newest accounts, as well as the average age of all your accounts.

A longer credit history gives lenders more information about your borrowing behavior. It's like a marathon runner with several races under their belt - their past performance indicates how they'll perform in future races.

While you can't speed up time to lengthen your credit history, you can make the most of it. Keep your oldest credit accounts open and in good standing to extend the length of your credit history. It's like a marathon runner keeping a steady pace, preserving their energy for the long haul.

Types of Credit Used: The Variety Pack of Credit

Finally, let's talk about the types of credit used. This refers to the mix of different credit accounts you have, including credit cards and other forms of debt like student loans, car loans, or a mortgage. It's like a variety pack of snacks - having a mix can make things more interesting!

Various credit types show lenders that you can handle different types of credit responsibly. It's like a musician who can play multiple instruments - it demonstrates versatility and skill.

While having every type of credit is unnecessary, and you should take on debt sparingly, managing your credit responsibly is essential. It's like playing each instrument in your repertoire with skill and finesse, creating a harmonious symphony.

And there we have it! We've explored the intricacies of credit cards, delved into strategies for using them wisely, and understood the impacts of credit card debt. We've also discussed how to build good credit early, from the importance of on-time payments to the benefits of keeping credit utilization low and the role of credit history length to the impact of the types of credit used. It's like understanding the rules of a complex game, mastering the strategies, and learning how to play wisely and responsibly.

As you stand at this juncture, equipped with your newfound knowledge and insights, remember this: Credit is a tool. It's neither good nor bad. It's how you use it that makes all the difference. So, wield this tool with wisdom, caution, and confidence. After all, your financial future isn't written in the cards; your hands shape it.

Now, turning the page, we'll move on to another significant aspect of personal finance that often weighs heavy on the minds of young adults – student loans. But fear not, for we'll tackle this topic together, breaking it down and making it approachable. So, brace yourself, for the adventure continues!

Ask the Captain

Captain, how do credit cards work? They seem like magic!

Ahoy, young sailor! Credit cards are like a double-edged sword. They let you borrow money to make purchases, acting as a short-term loan. But remember, this borrowed money needs to be paid back. If you pay it back within the billing cycle, it's smooth sailing. If you do, you'll avoid the rough seas of interest and fees.

What's the deal with credit card interest and fees, Captain?

Interest and fees are the winds and waves you face while navigating credit card waters. Interest, or APR, is the cost of borrowing money and kicks in if you don't pay your full balance. Fees can be for late payments, cash advances, or annual charges. It's crucial to understand these to avoid unnecessary costs.

Are credit card rewards really beneficial, Captain?

Credit card rewards can be like finding a treasure chest but must be used wisely. They offer cash back, redeemable points, or travel miles for your purchases. But beware lad, don't let the lure of rewards tempt you into spending more than you can afford. Always stick to your budget, even when chasing these rewards.

Captain, what are the risks of using a credit card irresponsibly?

Using a credit card without caution is like sailing into a storm. Overspending can lead to a mountain of debt, and missing payments can damage your credit score, making it hard to borrow money in the future. It's like a boat taking on water – if you're not careful, it can sink your financial ship.

How can I use my credit card wisely, Captain?

To use your credit card wisely is to navigate with a steady hand. Pay off your balance in full each month to avoid interest. Keep your credit utilization low – don't max out your card. And always pay on time to protect your credit score. It's like keeping your ship in top condition for the journey ahead.

What's the best way to avoid credit card debt, Captain?

Avoiding credit card debt requires discipline, like a seasoned sailor. Only charge what you can afford to pay off each month. Create a budget, stick to it, and track expenses to avoid overspending. It's like knowing the capacity of your ship and not overloading it.

Finally, how can I make sure my credit card helps instead of hurts my finances, Captain?

To make your credit card a helpful tool, you must master your financial ship. Use it for convenience, not as an extension of your income. Please take advantage of rewards, but don't let them steer your spending. Pay off balances in full and sail smoothly through your financial waters.

The Captain's Guiding Light: Navigating Credit Cards
(Key Chapter Takeaways)

1. **Credit Cards as a Financial Tool:** Credit cards are versatile tools that allow borrowing up to a certain limit for purchases or cash withdrawals. Managing them responsibly is crucial to avoid potential harm.

2. **Understanding Interest Rates and Fees:** Be aware of the costs associated with credit cards, including interest rates (APR) and various fees, which can significantly impact overall expenses.

3. **Rewards and Perks of Credit Cards:** Credit cards offer benefits like cashback, travel miles, and exclusive perks, which can be advantageous if used wisely without encouraging overspending.

4. **Potential Risks of Credit Cards:** Risks include the temptation to overspend, accruing high-interest debt, damaging credit scores, and increased vulnerability to identity theft.

5. **Paying Balances in Full:** Regularly paying off credit card balances in full each month avoids interest charges and positively impacts your credit score.

6. **Responsible Credit Limit Utilization:** Keep credit utilization (balance-to-limit ratio) below 30% to demonstrate responsible borrowing and positively impact credit scores.

7. **Avoiding Late Payments:** Late payments incur fees and damage credit scores. Set up automatic payments or reminders to ensure timely payments.

8. **Maximizing Credit Card Rewards:** Understand and utilize your card's rewards program for benefits, but avoid letting rewards incentives lead to overspending.

9. **Impact of Credit Card Debt on Credit Score:** Credit card debt can significantly lower credit scores, affecting future loan eligibility and interest rates.

10. **Emotional and Financial Toll of Credit Card Debt:** Debt can cause stress, anxiety, and affect personal relationships and mental health, in addition to long-term financial consequences like increased overall costs and reduced savings potential.

11. **Strategies for Building Good Credit Early:** Establish a positive credit history through on-time payments, low credit utilization, a long credit history,

and a variety of credit types to demonstrate financial responsibility and versatility to lenders.

12. **Navigating Credit Cards Wisely:** Using credit cards wisely involves understanding and managing their features, rewards, and potential pitfalls, much like mastering a complex game with strategic planning and responsible play.

Guiding Light in Your Financial Journey

"Like a lighthouse guiding ships through stormy seas, this book aims to illuminate your path in the world of money management."

As you reach the midpoint of **"Essential Money Skills for Teens,"** it's time to pause and reflect on the journey so far. Navigating the waters of financial responsibility might seem daunting, but remember, every great sailor once faced the same uncertainty.

Your Thoughts Matter!

Share your experience so far:

- What new insights have you gained?
- How has your perspective on money management changed?
- What chapters have resonated with you the most?

Your feedback is like fuel for our lighthouse, helping others find their way. Drop a review on Amazon and share your journey!

https://qrco.de/beYhae

Keep Sailing Forward!

There's more to explore and learn. Let's continue this voyage together, with our lighthouse guiding us through the exciting world of financial literacy.

CHAPTER SIX

STUDENT LOANS - A DOUBLE-EDGED SWORD

I magine coming ashore on a new island and standing at the edge of a vast forest. You're about to embark on a hike with breathtaking views, an adrenaline rush, and a sense of accomplishment. But the path is steep, the terrain challenging, and the journey long. Yet, you take that first step because you know the reward will be worth the struggle. This is what venturing into the world of student loans can feel like. It's a path that can lead to the enriching experience of higher education, yet it's fraught with complexities and potential pitfalls.

In this chapter, we'll guide you through this dense forest. We'll help you understand the different types of student loans, the terms and conditions that come with them, and how they are disbursed and used. This knowledge will equip you to confidently navigate the student loan landscape, making informed decisions that align with your financial goals and aspirations. So, let's lace up our hiking boots and start this trek.

6.1 AN OVERVIEW OF STUDENT LOANS

Federal vs. Private Student Loans: The Two Main Trails

Student loans can be categorized into two types: federal and private. Think of these as two main trails leading up the mountain.

The government provides federal student loans. They often come with lower interest rates and more flexible repayment options than private loans. They also offer benefits like loan forgiveness for public service work or income-driven repayment plans. However, you must meet specific eligibility criteria to access federal student loans and complete the Free Application for Federal Student Aid (FAFSA).

Private student loans are offered by private lenders like banks, credit unions, and online lenders. They are used to fill the funding gap if you need more than federal loans, grants, and scholarships to cover your education costs. Private loans may offer higher loan limits but often have higher interest rates and less flexible repayment options than federal loans.

Interest Rates and Repayment Terms: The Hike's Incline and Duration

Interest rates and repayment terms are crucial aspects of student loans. They determine how steep your climb will be (the cost of borrowing) and how long you'll be hiking (the repayment period).

The interest rate is the cost of borrowing money, expressed as a percentage of the loan amount. It's like the incline of your hike - the higher the rate, the steeper the climb. Federal student loans usually have fixed interest rates, meaning the rate stays the same throughout the life of the loan. Private student loans, on the other hand, can have fixed or variable rates. Variable rates can change over time, making your climb steeper or easier, depending on interest rate trends.

The repayment terms determine how long you'll repay your student loans. It's like the duration of your hike. Federal student loans generally have a standard repayment term of ten years, but this can be extended with specific repayment plans.

Private student loan repayment terms can vary widely by lender. Remember, a longer repayment term can make each payment more manageable, but you'll end up paying more in interest over the life of the loan.

Loan Disbursement and Use: The Trailhead and Path

The disbursement of a student loan is when the funds are sent from the lender to your school. It's like the starting point of your hike. Federal student loans are typically disbursed twice a year at the start of each term. The funds go first toward tuition, fees, room and board, and other school charges. If any money is left over, it will be refunded to you to be used for other education-related expenses.

The use of student loan funds is typically restricted to education-related expenses. This includes tuition, room and board, books, supplies, equipment, transportation, and educational expenses. It's like the marked trail you're supposed to follow on your hike.

Understanding these aspects of student loans can help you navigate your way toward a decision that aligns with your needs and circumstances. The path is challenging, and the hike can be strenuous. But with knowledge as your compass and careful planning as your map, you can successfully navigate the student loan landscape and reach the summit of your educational goals.

6.2 THE PROS AND CONS OF TAKING A STUDENT LOAN

Access to Higher Education: The Golden Ticket

Think of a student loan as a golden ticket. It opens the gates to the amusement park of higher education, allowing you to hop on the rollercoaster ride toward a degree. Without this ticket, the hefty price of admission might keep many potential students standing outside the park with dreams of higher education tantalizingly out of reach.

Student loans can cover various expenses, from tuition and fees to room and board, books, and other education-related costs. It's like having a season pass that gives you access to all the rides in the park. This financial support can make the difference between attending college or not, between pursuing a desired field of study or settling for a less preferred option.

Financial Responsibility and Discipline: A Crash Course in Money Management

Taking on a student loan is like enrolling in a crash course in financial responsibility. It's a real-world class that teaches you about interest rates, repayment schedules, and the long-term effects of debt.

You'll learn invaluable lessons about budgeting, saving, and financial planning as you navigate borrowing, repaying, and managing your student loan. It's like learning to drive a car. It can be nerve-wracking, with many rules to remember and skills to master. But with time and practice, you become a confident driver, skillfully navigating the financial highway.

Long-Term Debt Burden: The Heavy Backpack

A student loan can feel like a heavy backpack that you must carry long after you've left campus. This debt's weight can significantly burden your financial future, slowing your pace as you embark on your career and personal life.

This long-term debt burden can affect your ability to save money, invest for the future, or make large purchases like a car or a house. It's like trying to run a race with a heavy backpack. You can still move forward, but it's harder, slower, and requires more effort.

Impact on Future Financial Decisions: The Ripple Effect

Lastly, a student loan can create ripples that affect your future financial decisions. It's like throwing a stone into a pond. The splash might initially seem small, but the ripples spread, reaching far and wide.

Your student loan debt and your track record of repaying it will become part of your credit history, affecting your credit score and ability to borrow money. It might impact your career choice, pushing you towards higher-paying jobs to manage your loan repayments. It might delay other life goals, like starting a family or buying a home.

Taking a student loan is a significant decision that can have far-reaching consequences. It can provide you with the means to pursue higher education and teach you valuable lessons about financial responsibility. But it also comes with a long-term debt burden that can impact your future financial decisions and personal life. It's a path that requires careful consideration, informed decisions, and diligent management. Rest assured, with the proper knowledge and tools, you can successfully navigate this path, turning your higher education dreams into a reality.

6.3 MANAGING STUDENT LOANS EFFECTIVELY

Understanding Your Loan Agreement: Decoding the Contract

Think of a student loan agreement as a map given before a treasure hunt. It outlines the rules, the route you should take, and the steps needed to claim your prize. The agreement includes essential information about your loan, such as the loan amount, interest rate, repayment terms, and your rights and responsibilities as a borrower.

The loan amount is the treasure you receive to fund your education. The interest rate is like the ticking clock, adding to your debt as time passes. The lender is the organizer of this treasure hunt, and you, the borrower, are the participant, navigating the path to successful loan repayment.

Knowing the details of your loan agreement is crucial. It helps you anticipate what lies ahead and plan your moves wisely. Therefore, take the time to read and understand your loan agreement. Ask questions if anything needs to be clarified. It's your game, but you must know the rules to play it well.

Making Regular Payments: Staying on Track

In the treasure hunt of student loans, making regular payments is equivalent to promptly following the clues. Each payment brings you closer to the ultimate treasure - being debt-free.

Your loan agreement will outline when you need to start making payments and how much they will be. Some loans require you to begin repayment while you're still in school, while others offer a grace period, allowing you to start repayment after graduation.

Setting up automatic payments can ensure you get all the due dates. It's like having a compass that always points you in the right direction. Prompt payments can boost your credit score and save you from late fees or increased interest charges. It's a surefire strategy to stay on track in your student loan treasure hunt.

Exploring Repayment Plans: Choosing the Right Path

The road to repaying student loans isn't a one-way street. There are different paths you can take, known as repayment plans. Choosing the right plan is like deciding between taking the quickest or the most scenic route in a race.

Federal student loans offer several repayment plans, including standard, graduated, and extended repayment plans. There are also income-driven repayment plans, where your monthly payment is based on your income and family size.

On the other hand, private lenders usually have less flexible repayment options. However, some may offer flexibility, such as graduated repayment or interest-only payments for a certain period.

Consider your financial situation and long-term goals when choosing a repayment plan. Remember, you can switch plans if your circumstances change. It's your race to run, and you get to choose the path.

Loan Forgiveness Programs: The Shortcut to the Finish Line

In the race for student loan repayment, loan forgiveness programs are like hidden shortcuts. They offer a path to have some or all of your loan debt forgiven under certain conditions.

Public Service Loan Forgiveness (PSLF) is one such program for federal student loans. If you work full-time for a qualifying employer, usually a government or non-profit organization, and make 120 qualifying payments, the remaining balance of your loan is forgiven.

Teacher Loan Forgiveness is another program specifically for teachers employed full-time in a low-income school or educational service agency for five consecutive years.

Remember, these programs have specific requirements and conditions; not everyone will qualify. But if you do, they can provide a significant boost in your race towards being debt-free.

Navigating the world of student loans can be complex, but with the proper knowledge and strategies, you can effectively manage your loans. From understanding your loan agreement to making regular payments, from choosing the right repayment plan to exploring loan forgiveness programs, you can chart your path toward successful loan repayment. Remember, this isn't just a race against debt. It's a journey toward financial independence and realizing your educational dreams. So, keep going, one step at a time, one payment at a time. You're doing great, and you've got this!

6.4 EXPLORING ALTERNATIVES TO STUDENT LOANS

Scholarships and Grants: The Golden Goose

Let's start with scholarships and grants, the golden goose for college financing. Unlike loans, these funds do not need to be repaid – they're free money for your education. Scholarships are usually merit-based, awarded for academic or athletic achievements, while grants are typically need-based, given to students with financial need.

To find scholarships and grants, start with your school's financial aid office, then expand your search to local community organizations, businesses, and online scholarship databases. Apply for as many as possible – every dollar you receive is less than you'll need in loans. It's like finding golden eggs – the more you see, the richer your nest.

Work-Study Programs: Earning While Learning

Work-study programs are another alternative to student loans. They allow students to earn money to help cover education expenses while gaining valuable work experience. It's like having a part-time job but with a twist – the money you earn is specifically for your education costs.

Federal Work-Study provides part-time jobs for undergraduate and graduate students with financial need. Jobs can be on-campus or off-campus, and students are paid at least the federal minimum wage. Many schools also offer work-study programs, so check with your financial aid office for opportunities.

Saving and Investing for College: Planting Seeds for the Future

Another alternative to student loans is saving and investing for college ahead of time. It's like planting and nurturing a seed over time, watching it grow into a money tree. Starting a college savings fund early and contributing to it regularly can accumulate a significant amount over time.

One popular option is a 529 college savings plan, which offers tax advantages for college savings. Another option is a Coverdell Education Savings Account, which can be used for college and K-12 education expenses.

Community College or Trade School Options: The Road Less Traveled

Community colleges or trade schools can be less expensive than four-year colleges and universities. They offer associate degrees, certificates, and vocational training programs that can lead to rewarding careers. It's a shorter, less traveled road that can still lead to your desired destination – a successful career.

Many students start at a community college and then transfer to a four-year college to complete their bachelor's degree. This can significantly lower the overall cost of a degree.

Employer Tuition Assistance Programs: Climbing the Corporate Ladder

Finally, some employers offer tuition assistance programs as a part of their benefits package. They may reimburse you for tuition, fees, and books for courses related to your job. It's like climbing the rigging of your ship and finding treasures along the way.

Check with your human resources department to see if your employer offers this benefit. And remember, this assistance could be tax-deductible up to a certain amount.

There you have it! There are many alternatives to student loans, from scholarships and grants to work-study programs, from saving and investing to community college and employer tuition assistance programs. They're like different paths leading to the same destination – a college education. By exploring these paths, you can find a route that fits your needs, minimizes debt, and leads you toward a bright financial future. As we continue our adventure into personal finance, we'll explore another crucial aspect that often accompanies student loans – credit and debt management. Let's keep moving forward, armed with the knowledge we've gained and eager to learn more.

Ask the Captain

Captain, what's the difference between federal and private student loans?

Ahoy, mate! Consider federal student loans like a sturdy, government-supplied vessel – often with lower interest rates and more flexible payment options. They're the safer bet for most sailors. Private student loans are more like speedy, privateer ships offered by banks or other companies. They might provide more money, but usually at higher interest rates and less favorable terms. Navigate wisely!

How do interest rates and repayment terms work with student loans, Captain?

Interest rates on student loans are like the currents of the sea – they affect how smoothly your financial voyage goes. Federal loans often have fixed rates, steady as the North Star, while private loans can have variable rates, as unpredictable as the tides. Repayment terms set the length of your journey – longer terms might make monthly payments more manageable, but you'll pay more interest over time.

What about loan disbursement and use, Captain? How does that work?

When your student loan is disbursed, it's like your ship being loaded with supplies at port. The funds cover your college's tuition and room and board expenses. Any leftover is like extra provisions you can use for other education-related costs. Remember, this treasure is for your educational voyage only, not for other adventures!

Are student loans really a good idea, Captain? What are the risks?

Student loans are like setting sail on a long voyage – they can lead to new horizons but come with risks. They provide access to the treasure of education but also mean taking on debt you'll have to repay with interest. It's a commitment, like signing on for a long journey at sea. It would help if you were sure you're ready for the responsibility and the long-term impact on your financial health.

How do I manage my student loans effectively, Captain?

Managing your student loans is like navigating through treacherous waters. Understand your loan agreement – it's your map. Make regular payments – they're your steady winds keeping you on course. Choose the right repayment plan – it's like choosing the correct route – and explore forgiveness programs if you qualify – they can be like finding a shortcut. Stay disciplined and keep your eyes on the horizon!

Are there alternatives to student loans, Captain? How do I find them?

Aye, there are other routes to funding your education, like finding treasure islands along your voyage. Look for scholarships and grants – they're like finding chests of gold that you don't have to repay. Work-study programs offer the chance to earn as you learn. Consider community college or trade school for a more affordable path. And don't forget employer tuition assistance – some captains are willing to invest in their crew's education!

Any final advice for navigating student loans, Captain?

Keep a sharp eye on the horizon and a steady hand on the wheel. Use student loans wisely – don't borrow more than you need or can handle. Remember that this debt will be with you for a while, like a constant companion on your journey. Plan for it, manage it well, and it can be a valuable tool in reaching the shores of your educational goals!

The Captain's Guiding Light: Student Loans (Key Chapter Takeaways)

1. **Understanding Federal vs. Private Student Loans:** Know the differences between federal loans, which often have lower interest rates and more flexible repayment options, and private loans, which may fill funding gaps but typically have higher interest rates.

2. **Interest Rates and Repayment Terms:** Interest rates determine the cost of borrowing, and repayment terms set the loan's duration. Federal loans usually have fixed rates, while private loans can have variable rates.

3. **Disbursement and Usage of Loan Funds:** Loans are usually disbursed to the school first for tuition and fees, with any surplus given to the student for other education-related expenses.

4. **Pros and Cons of Student Loans:** Access to higher education and financial discipline are significant advantages, but they come with the risk of a long-term debt burden and potential impact on future financial decisions.

5. **Managing Student Loans Effectively:** Understand loan agreements, make regular payments,

choose the right repayment plan, and explore loan forgiveness programs to manage loans responsibly.

6. **Alternatives to Student Loans:** Investigate scholarships, grants, work-study programs, savings plans, community college or trade school options, and employer tuition assistance to reduce or avoid student loan debt.

7. **The Role of Student Loans in Accessing Higher Education:** Loans can be essential in making higher education attainable, providing opportunities for academic and career advancement.

8. **Long-Term Financial Planning with Student Loans:** Consider the impact of student loans on long-term financial goals, including saving, investing, and major life decisions.

9. **Credit Implications of Student Loans:** Student loan management affects credit scores, influencing future borrowing opportunities and terms.

10. **Navigating the Student Loan Landscape:** Armed with knowledge and understanding, students can navigate the complexities of student loans, making informed decisions that align with their educational and financial goals.

CHAPTER SEVEN

INVESTING - NOT JUST FOR THE RICH AND FAMOUS

Picture this: you're at a carnival. The scene is electric with excitement; the scent of popcorn fills the air, and you're standing in front of a brightly lit game booth. You're handed three small rings to toss onto a pyramid of glass bottles. It doesn't seem easy, but with each toss, you realize there is a technique to get it right. Investing is a lot like that carnival game. It might initially seem intimidating, but it can be a fun and rewarding experience once you understand the technique.

In this chapter, we'll dive into the exciting world of investing. We'll uncover the basics, marvel once again at the magic of compound interest, and understand the importance of diversification. So, roll up your sleeves, take a deep breath, and let's get ready to toss our first ring!

7.1: INTRODUCTION TO INVESTING

The Basics of Investing: Learning the Rules of the Game

Investing is putting your money into various financial instruments, such as stocks, bonds, or mutual funds, hoping to make a profit. It's like buying a ticket for the roller coaster rather than the merry-go-round, knowing there may be ups and downs on the ride but also that the thrill and potential make it worth it.

There are two primary ways you can make money from investing. The first is when the investment increases in value, and you sell it for more than what you paid – this is called capital gains. It's like hitting the bullseye in a dart game and winning the grand prize. The second way is through income from the investment, such as interest or dividends. It's like those minor prizes you win along the way to the big reward, keeping you motivated to play the game.

The Power of Compound Interest: The Roller Coaster Ride

Remember the snowball effect in the savings chapter? Well, brace yourself because we're about to explore that exhilarating concept again, this time in investing. Compound interest in investing works much the same way as it does with a savings account. The difference is that the potential returns from investments are generally higher than from a regular savings account, which means the snowball can grow larger over time.

Let's consider an example. Suppose you invest $1000 in a mutual fund that averages a 7% return annually. In the first year, you'd earn $70 in interest. In the second year, you'd earn interest not only on your original $1000 but also on the $70 you earned in the first year. That means, in the second year, you'd earn about $74.90 in interest, bringing your total to $1144.90. Over time, your investment continues to grow, from your principal amount and the interest it earns each year. It's like being on a roller coaster that gradually climbs higher and higher, with each loop more exciting than the last.

The Importance of Diversification: Don't Put All Your Rings in One Basket

Let's go back to that carnival game booth. Would you throw all your rings simultaneously, aiming for the same bottle? Probably not. You'd spread out your throws. That's diversification in the world of investing. It means spreading your investments across various financial instruments, industries, and geographical areas.

Why diversify? Because it helps reduce risk. Just like you wouldn't bet all your carnival tickets on one game, you don't want to put all your money into one investment. If one market sector goes down, but you're invested in various sectors, your overall risk is reduced.

Consider this scenario: Let's say you invest all your money in a company that makes cars. If that company goes bankrupt or the automobile industry takes a hit, you stand to lose a lot, maybe even all, of your investment. Let's say instead you spread your investments among a car company, a technology firm, a healthcare provider, and a consumer goods manufacturer. If the car company goes under, but the other companies do well, you still have a good chance of making a profit or at least not losing as much. That's diversification at work.

Investing is a game of chance, but it's far from a random toss. It requires understanding the basics, harnessing the power of compound interest, and diversifying your investments. With these strategies, you're not just tossing rings randomly in a carnival game; you're strategically aiming for financial growth.

7.2 UNDERSTANDING STOCKS, BONDS, AND MUTUAL FUNDS

Stocks: Ownership Shares in Companies

Now, let's take a closer look at some specific types of investments, starting with stocks. Buying a stock means buying a small piece of ownership in a company. It's like buying a slice of a giant pizza. The more slices (or stocks) you have, the bigger your share in the company.

When you own stock in a company, you become a shareholder, which often comes with the right to vote on certain company matters. It's like being part of a club and getting a say in decisions.

The value of a stock can go up or down depending on various factors like the company's performance, economic conditions, and investor sentiment. If the stock's value goes up and you sell your shares, you make a profit. But if the value decreases and you sell, you could lose money. It's like a roller coaster ride with potential highs and lows.

Bonds: Lending Money to Companies or Governments

On the other hand, bonds are like loans you give to a company or government. In return for your loan, the borrower promises to pay you interest regularly and return the principal amount on a specified date.

Let's go back to the pizza analogy. If stocks are like buying a slice of pizza, bonds are like lending money to your friend to buy a pizza. In return, your friend promises to pay you back with a little extra for your trouble.

Bonds are generally considered less risky than stocks because bondholders are paid before shareholders if a company goes bankrupt. However, the potential returns from bonds are also usually lower than stocks. Choosing bonds is like a gentle carousel ride over a thrilling roller coaster − less excitement and risk.

Mutual Funds: Pooled Investments

Mutual funds are like a big potluck party. Multiple investors pool their money together, and a professional fund manager uses that money to buy a diversified mix of stocks, bonds, or other assets.

Each investor owns shares in the mutual fund, representing a portion of the fund's holdings. It's like bringing a dish to a potluck and enjoying various food.

Investing in a mutual fund gives instant diversification and professional management of your money. However, mutual funds come with fees that can eat into your returns. It's like having a wide variety of food at a potluck but paying a fee for the organization and venue.

Understanding the different types of investments − stocks, bonds, and mutual funds − is like knowing the ins and outs of other carnival games. Each game has its rules, risks, and potential rewards. By understanding these, you can choose which games to play, know how to play them and increase your chances of winning.

7.3 THE CONCEPT OF RISK AND REWARD

Understanding Risk Tolerance: Setting Your Roller Coaster Limits

In investing, risk and reward are two sides of the same coin. Typically, investments with higher potential returns come with higher risk, while lower-risk investments offer lower potential returns. It's like choosing between a high-speed roller coaster and a gentle carousel ride at an amusement park.

Your risk tolerance is your ability to withstand losses in your investments. It's like your roller coaster limits. Some people can stomach the biggest, fastest roller coasters without flinching, while others prefer slower, gentler rides.

Your risk tolerance can depend on several factors, including financial goals, investment timeline, and personal comfort with risk. Before you invest, it's essential to understand your risk tolerance and choose investments that align with it.

Balancing Risk and Reward: The Art of Investing

Investing is all about balancing risk and reward. It's like walking a tightrope at the carnival. You want to get to the other side (your financial goals), but you must also stay balanced to avoid falling.

Higher-risk investments, like stocks, have the potential for higher returns and volatility. It's like a thrilling roller coaster ride with exhilarating highs and stomach-churning lows.

On the other hand, lower-risk investments, like bonds, offer more stability but typically lower returns. It's like a gentle carousel ride, steady and predictable.

A well-balanced investment portfolio includes a mix of different investments, which can help smooth out the ups and downs. It's like enjoying a variety of rides at the amusement park – the thrill of the roller coaster, the steadiness of the carousel, and everything in between.

The Role of Time in Investing Risk: The Timekeeper of Investing

Time plays a crucial role in investing. Generally, the longer you plan to keep your money invested, the more risk you can afford to take. It's like spending a whole day at the amusement park – you have time to try all the rides, even if some make you dizzy.

This is because, over the long term, the highs and lows of the market tend to even out, and the overall trend has historically been up. So, if you're investing for a long-term goal, like retirement, you can weather more ups and downs in your investments.

However, if your investment timeline is short, you'll want to take on less risk. It's like going to the amusement park just before closing time – you might stick to the rides you know you'll enjoy rather than chancing a ride that could leave you feeling queasy.

Understanding the relationship between risk and reward, knowing your risk tolerance, and considering the role of time in investment risk can help you make informed decisions in your investing journey. It's like having a map of the amusement park, knowing which rides you enjoy, and planning the day. With these tools, you're ready to navigate the investing landscape and make choices that align with your goals and comfort level.

7.4 INVESTING ON A SHOESTRING BUDGET

Micro-Investing Apps: The Piggy Bank Goes Digital

Think back to those childhood days when you would drop loose change into your piggy bank, joyfully rattling it now and then to hear the satisfying jingle of coins. That was micro-saving, and in today's digital age, it has evolved into micro-investing. Micro-investing apps have transformed the financial landscape, enabling you to invest spare change from everyday transactions.

Imagine buying a cup of coffee for $4.50. A micro-investing app rounds up the purchase to $5 and invests the spare 50 cents. The beauty of these apps lies in their simplicity and automation. They save and invest for you, turning your digital spare change into a growing investment portfolio. It's a small, steady step towards your financial goals, proving that every cent counts.

Regular Small Investments: The Slow and Steady Approach

Picture yourself as a diligent gardener, planting seeds regularly in your financial garden. Those seeds are small, regular investments that you make, regardless of the market conditions. This strategy, known as dollar-cost averaging, involves investing a fixed amount at regular intervals.

Here's how it works: Let's say you invest $50 monthly. Some months, when investment prices are low, your $50 buys more shares. Other months, when prices are high, the exact $50 buys fewer shares. Over time, this can lower the average cost of your investments.

The key to this approach is consistency. Like regularly watering your plants, making small investments can lead to a flourishing financial garden over time. It's a testament to the age-old saying: slow and steady wins the race.

Low-Cost Index Funds: The Economical Ride

Imagine boarding a train that takes you on a scenic tour of the financial market. This ride is akin to investing in low-cost index funds. An index fund is a type of mutual fund or exchange-traded fund (ETF) designed to track the performance of a specific market index, such as the S&P 500. Simply put, when investing in an index fund, you're investing in a broad cross-section of the market.

Why emphasize 'low-cost?' Because index funds are passively managed. They aim to mimic the market index performance they track, not outperform it. This means they don't require fund managers to analyze stocks and make buying or selling decisions, cutting management costs. Lower costs mean more of your money goes towards your investment rather than being eaten up by fees.

Index funds offer a simple, cost-effective way to diversify your investment portfolio. By buying a single index fund, you get a piece of hundreds or even thousands of companies. It's an economical ticket to a panoramic view of the market.

In the realm of investing, starting small doesn't mean thinking small. With micro-investing apps, regular small investments, and low-cost index funds, you can begin your investing journey with what you already have right where you are. Remember, it's not about the investment size but rather the habit of investing that makes the real difference. So, invest confidently, knowing that every small step is a leap toward your financial goals.

As we flip the page to the next chapter, we'll focus on another crucial aspect of financial literacy - planning for big-ticket items. Whether saving for a new car, a dream home, or your education, planning is critical to making those dreams a reality. So, get ready to take your financial planning skills to the next level. Onward and upward we go!

Ask the Captain

Captain, how does one start with investing? It doesn't seem very easy.

Ahoy, young navigator! Investing is like learning to sail. Start by understanding the basics – stocks, bonds, and mutual funds. Stocks are like owning a part of a ship, bonds are like lending money for a ship's voyage, and mutual funds are like owning a mix of different vessels. Begin with a small amount, learn the ropes, and gradually increase your investment as you gain confidence.

What's this 'compound interest' in investing, Captain?

Compound interest in investing, matey, is like a favorable wind that grows stronger over time, carrying your ship farther than expected. It's not just the money you invest that earns a return, but also the returns on those returns. Over time, this compounding effect can significantly increase the value of your investment, like a snowball growing as it rolls down a hill.

Is diversification really important in investing, Captain?

Lad! diversification is like having a fleet of different ships. If a storm hits and one ship struggles, the others can continue the voyage unharmed. By spreading your investments across different types – such as stocks, bonds, and real estate – you reduce the risk of all your investments being affected by the same adverse condition.

Captain, what are the risks and rewards of investing?

Every investment, like every sea voyage, carries risk and potential reward. Higher-risk investments, like stocks, can lead to higher rewards but also higher losses. Safer investments, like bonds, typically offer lower returns but also lower risk. Your job as an investor is to balance risk and reward based on your financial goals and how much risk you're comfortable taking.

How can I invest if I don't have much money, Captain?

You don't need a full treasure chest to start investing, young sailor! Micro-investing apps allow you to invest small amounts – even spare change from daily transactions. Regular small investments can build up over time. Additionally, low-cost index funds are a great way to start with minimal funds. It's about making consistent, small contributions, not about starting big.

Can you explain stocks, bonds, and mutual funds in simple terms, Captain?

Stocks are like buying a piece of a company – if the company does well, your share increases in value. Bonds are like lending money to a company or government – in return for you loaning it to them, they pay you interest and eventually repay the entire loan. Mutual funds combine stocks, bonds, and other investments – like a collection of different maritime ventures in one investment.

What should I consider when it comes to risk in investing, Captain?

Consider your risk tolerance – how much financial turbulence you can comfortably handle. Higher risks can lead to higher rewards, but they can also lead to more significant losses. Your age, financial goals, and investment timeframe are crucial in determining how much risk you should take. Like a long voyage, the more time you have, the more risks you can potentially afford.

How does one invest on a shoestring budget, Captain?

You can set sail in the investing sea even with a small budget! Use micro-investing apps to start small, invest in low-cost index funds for broad market exposure, and consider regular small investments over time. It's like gathering resources bit by bit to prepare for a grand voyage.

❄

The Captain's Guiding Light: Investing
(Key Chapter Takeaways)

1. **Investing Fundamentals:** Investing involves allocating money into various financial instruments like stocks, bonds, or mutual funds to earn profits, akin to playing a strategic carnival game.
2. **The Role of Compound Interest:** Compound interest in investing accelerates profit growth over time, similar to a snowball effect, making early and consistent investments advantageous.
3. **Diversification Strategy:** Diversifying investments across different financial instruments and markets reduces risk, much like spreading out attempts in a carnival game.
4. **Stocks, Bonds, and Mutual Funds:** Understanding these investment types is crucial; stocks offer ownership in companies, bonds act as loans with interest, and mutual funds pool money for diversified investments.
5. **Risk and Reward Balance:** Investing involves balancing risk (potential losses) with reward (potential gains), necessitating an understanding of personal risk tolerance and investment time horizon.
6. **Micro-Investing Apps:** These apps allow investing small, spare changes from daily transactions, making investing accessible and manageable on any budget.
7. **Regular Small Investments:** Consistently investing small amounts (dollar-cost averaging) can

lead to significant growth over time, demonstrating the power of steady, disciplined investing.

8. **Low-Cost Index Funds:** Index funds offer a cost-effective and straightforward way to diversify investments, tracking broad market indices with lower management fees.

9. **Investment on a Shoestring Budget:** Even with limited funds, smart investment strategies like micro-investing, consistent small contributions, and low-cost index funds can build a robust investment portfolio.

10. **Investment as an Accessible Financial Tool:** Investing is not exclusively for the wealthy; with the right knowledge and tools, anyone can start investing and grow their financial resources.

CHAPTER EIGHT

PLANNING FOR BIG-TICKET ITEMS: YOUR FUTURE STARTS NOW

I magine standing at the base of a towering mountain, its peak hidden in the clouds. You're about to climb this mountain, one that represents your big-ticket financial goals. It's a bit daunting. But don't worry; you won't make this climb unprepared. With the right tools and strategies, you'll conquer these heights and the view at the top. It's going to be spectacular.

8.1 SAVING FOR COLLEGE: THE OPTIONS

529 College Savings Plans: Your Financial GPS

Think of a 529 College Savings Plan as a GPS for your educational journey. It's a state or institution-sponsored savings plan designed to encourage saving for future education costs. Named after Section 529 of the Internal Revenue Code, these plans offer tax-free earnings growth and tax-free withdrawals when the funds are used for qualified education expenses. It's like driving on a toll-free highway where your journey toward your education goal becomes more accessible.

Different states offer various 529 plans, each with unique features, and you're not restricted to using your own state's plan. It's like having multiple GPS routes to reach your destination. You can choose the one that best suits your needs.

Coverdell Education Savings Accounts: The Versatile Vehicle

On the other hand, a Coverdell education savings account (ESA) is like a versatile vehicle, ready to take you to any educational destination. It's a trust or custodial account designed specifically for paying qualified education expenses for college and elementary and high school.

The benefit of a Coverdell ESA is the wide range of qualified expenses, including tuition, books, supplies, and even computer technology. It's like having an all-terrain vehicle that can navigate various paths of the education landscape.

However, there are contribution limits to consider. Under the current law, you can contribute up to $2,000 per year to a Coverdell ESA, which is not tax-deductible. But, similar to a 529 plan, your investment grows tax-free, and withdrawals for qualified education expenses are also tax-free.

Scholarships and Grants: The Golden Tickets of Education

Scholarships and grants are like golden tickets, offering free rides toward your college education. These are sums of money awarded to students that don't need to be repaid. It's like finding a treasure chest on your journey, easing your burden significantly.

Scholarships are typically based on merit. They're awarded for academic or athletic achievements and other specific criteria set by the scholarship provider. It's like being rewarded for exceptional performance in a sports tournament.

Grants are typically need-based and provided to students who demonstrate financial need. The federal government, state governments, and many colleges and universities offer grants. It's like receiving a care package when you're in need.

To maximize these golden opportunities, you'll start your search early and apply for as many scholarships and grants as possible. It's like participating in multiple raffles to increase your chances of winning a prize.

Your climb towards big-ticket items like a college education might seem steep, but with tools like 529 plans, Coverdell ESAs, scholarships, and grants, you're equipped for the ascent. These financial instruments, like trusty climbing tools, will help you navigate the rocky terrain of education expenses. So, gear up, take a deep breath, and take that first step. The peak awaits, and the view from the top is going to be worth it.

8.2 PLANNING FOR YOUR FIRST CAR

Saving for a Down Payment: The Foundation of Your Dream

Picture yourself at the starting line of a race, with the finish line being your shiny new car. The first stride you must take in this race is saving for a down payment. This initial cash outlay lowers the amount you need to borrow and paves the way for lower monthly payments. It's like the starter's pistol in a race, setting you off on the right foot.

How much should you save for a down payment? Aim for at least 20% of the car's price. It's like setting a solid pace right from the start - it may seem challenging, but it sets you up for success later on. Create a dedicated savings account for this purpose, and consider setting up automatic transfers to make the process smoother. It's like having a dedicated lane in your race, keeping you focused on your goal.

Understanding Auto Loans: Navigating the Financial Highway

The next step in your race to car ownership is understanding auto loans. These loans give you the funds to buy your car, which you pay back over a set period with interest. It's like the marked route of your race, guiding your path toward the finish line.

Consider the loan term, interest rate, and monthly payments when exploring auto loan options. A shorter loan term means higher monthly payments but less interest over the life of the loan. On the other hand, a longer term means lower monthly payments, but you'll pay more in interest overall. It's like choosing between the shorter, steeper route or the longer, gentler path in your race - each has pros and cons.

The interest rate on your auto loan can depend on various factors, including your credit score, the loan term, and whether the car is new or used. Shop around and compare loan offers to ensure you get the best deal. It's like scouting the race terrain beforehand, ensuring no unexpected obstacles.

The Costs of Car Ownership: Beyond the Finish Line

Crossing the finish line and getting your car keys is a thrilling moment. But remember, the race doesn't end there. The ongoing costs of car ownership are like the cool-down after the race - they're part of the process, even if they're not the most exciting part.

These costs include car insurance, which is legally required in most states. The insurance cost can depend on factors like your age, driving record, and the type of car you have. It's like the water station after a race, replenishing your resources and keeping you on track.

Consistent maintenance and repairs are also part of car ownership. Regular oil changes, tire rotations, and brake inspections can keep your car running smoothly and prevent costly repairs. It's like the post-race stretches that keep your muscles limber and prevent injuries.

Finally, remember fuel costs and vehicle registration fees. These recurring costs are part of the journey of car owner-ship. They're like the regular training that maintains your fitness level after the race.

Planning for your first car is like preparing for and running a race. It requires setting a goal, training consistently, under-standing the route, and persevering until the finish line. And even after the race, the journey continues with regular training and fitness maintenance. With this roadmap, you're ready to sprint towards your dream of car ownership, one stride at a time. So, strap on your running shoes, take a deep breath, and set your sights on the finish line. Your dream car awaits!

8.3 DREAMING OF HOME OWNERSHIP

The Process of Buying a Home: Mapping Out the Route

Envision standing at the edge of a labyrinth, a complex network of paths leading to your dream home at the center. The path to homeownership can feel like navigating a maze filled with twists, turns, and occasional dead ends. But fear not; with a clear map and a steady stride, you can find your way to the heart of this maze - your new home.

The first step is determining your budget. This involves looking hard at your income, expenses, savings, and debt. It's about understanding how much home you can afford without straining your finances. Picture it as the boundary line of the labyrinth, guiding you on a path that's within your means.

Next, you'll want to get pre-approved for a mortgage. This involves a lender checking your financial background and determining how much they'd be willing to lend you. It's like having a torchlight in the labyrinth, illuminating your path and making your journey easier.

Once pre-approved, you can start shopping for homes within your budget. This is where the fun begins! It's time to explore different neighborhoods, tour prospective houses, and imagine your life in each space. It's a thrilling labyrinth exploration, leading you closer to the center with each step.

After finding a home you love, you'll make an offer. If the seller accepts, the house goes into escrow, which is a period when all the legal and financial details are sorted out. It's the last leg of the labyrinth, with the center - your dream home - within sight.

Saving for a Down Payment: Building Your Financial Ladder

Now, let's talk about one of the most critical steps in the home-buying process - saving for a down payment. It's like building a sturdy ladder that will help you scale the wall to home-ownership.

A down payment is a percentage of the home's purchase price that you pay upfront. It reduces the amount you need to borrow and can lower your monthly mortgage payments. It's a powerful rung in your financial ladder, providing solid footing as you climb.

Experts often recommend a down payment of 20% of the home's price. However, many lenders offer loans with lower down payment requirements, especially for first-time home-buyers. It's like choosing between a tall ladder and a short one. Both can get you over the wall, but the taller ladder makes the climb a bit easier.

Consider setting up a dedicated savings account and making regular deposits to save for a down payment. Trim unnecessary expenses, increase your income with side gigs, or invest to grow your savings faster. Each dollar saved is another rung added to your ladder, bringing you one step closer to your dream home.

Understanding Mortgages: The Key to Your New Home

Finally, let's demystify mortgages - the key that unlocks the door to your new home. A mortgage is a loan used to purchase a home, with the house as collateral.

Mortgages come with an interest rate, the cost you pay to borrow the money. Some mortgages have a fixed interest rate, which stays the same over the life of the loan. Others have an adjustable rate, which changes periodically. It's like choosing a key with a straight or serrated edge. Both can open the lock, but they work in different ways.

The loan term is the time you have to repay the loan. Most mortgages have a term of fifteen or thirty years. A shorter term means higher monthly payments but less interest paid over the life of the loan. A longer-term means lower monthly payments but more interest paid over time. It's like having a choice of two keys - a regular key or a skeleton key. Both can unlock the door, but they offer different experiences.

Understanding the process of buying a home, saving for a down payment, and navigating the world of mortgages can make the labyrinth of homeownership less daunting. With each step, you're not just getting closer to buying a home. You're building financial savvy, understanding complex processes, and making decisions that will shape your life. It's not just about the destination but also about the growth and learning that happens along the way. So, take that first step into the labyrinth, map in hand, and let's find our way to your dream home, one turn at a time.

8.4 THE IMPORTANCE OF AN EMERGENCY FUND

Why You Need an Emergency Fund: Your Financial Safety Net

Picture yourself on a trapeze, soaring high above the ground in a dazzling display of agility and strength. Imagine doing all those flips and swings without a safety net below. Sounds scary, right? In personal finance, an emergency fund is that safety net. It's a stash of money to cover unexpected expenses or financial emergencies.

Life can be unpredictable, throwing us curveballs like job loss, medical emergencies, or car repairs. These unexpected expenses can throw your budget off balance and lead to debt if you need to prepare. That's where an emergency fund steps in. It provides a financial buffer, allowing you to cover these costs without dipping into your regular income or savings. It's like having a safety net that catches you when you fall, preventing a financial tumble.

How Much to Save: Your Personal Safety Cushion

So, how big should your safety net be? The size of your emergency fund can depend on various factors, including your monthly expenses, income stability, and personal comfort level. However, a good rule of thumb is to aim for three to six months of living expenses. This gives you a substantial buffer to weather most financial storms.

Think of it like packing for a camping trip. You wouldn't just pack food and clothes for one day. You'd pack enough supplies to last the entire trip and a bit extra for emergencies. Similarly, your emergency fund should be robust enough to see you through a few months of financial hardship.

Where to Keep Your Emergency Fund: Your Financial First Aid Kit

Finally, let's talk about where to keep your emergency fund. It should be easily accessible but not so accessible that you're tempted to dip into it for everyday expenses. Think of it as storing away extra supplies for your journey. You wouldn't use them when you have plenty of food, right? You'd save them a real emergency.

A high-yield savings account is an excellent option for your emergency fund. These accounts offer higher interest rates than regular savings accounts, allowing your money to grow while it sits. Plus, they provide easy access to your money when you need it.

Avoid investing your emergency fund in the stock market or other high-risk investments. The value of these investments can fluctuate, and you risk losing your safety net when you need it most. It's like packing a deflated life raft for a boating trip - it will only be a little help in an emergency.

Building an emergency fund might not be as thrilling as saving for a new car or a dream vacation, but it's crucial to financial health. The safety net catches you when life trips you up, the first aid kit that patches up financial wounds, and the life raft that keeps you afloat in a sea of unexpected expenses. It's not just about the money you save but the peace of mind that comes with knowing you're prepared for whatever life throws your way.

As we wrap up this chapter, take a moment to reflect on what you've learned. From saving for college to planning for your first car, from dreaming of homeownership to building an emergency fund, these lessons equip you with the tools you need to navigate the financial landscape confidently. They empower you to take charge of your financial future, one dollar, one decision, and one step at a time. So, keep learning, keep growing, and keep moving forward. You're on the path to financial success, and every step you take brings you closer to your goals. Next, we will explore another critical financial planning facet: the money mindset.

Ask the Captain

Captain, how do I start saving for college? It seems like such a huge expense!

Ahoy, young sailor! Begin with setting your course using tools like 529 college savings plans or Coverdell education savings accounts. These are like your navigational maps, guiding you towards your goal with tax advantages. Also, scout for scholarships and grants – these are like favorable winds that can propel your journey forward without weighing down your financial ship.

What about buying my first car, Captain? How do I navigate that?

To purchase your first vessel – I mean, car – start by saving for a down payment, just like you would gather supplies before a long voyage. Aim for at least 20% of the car's price. Then, understand auto loans – like the currents that can push your boat forward. And don't forget to consider the ongoing costs of car ownership, like maintenance and insurance. It's not just about getting the car but also about keeping it seaworthy.

Captain, what should I know about buying a home? It feels like setting sail on a vast ocean!

Buying a home is indeed a grand voyage, mate! Start by charting your budget to understand what you can afford – this is your compass. Then, get pre-approved for a mortgage, like getting your ship ready for the journey. Remember, the down payment is your anchor, providing stability. Research neighborhoods and home prices like studying the sea charts, and when you find your dream home, make an offer as if you're choosing the best course to navigate.

How much should I save in my emergency fund, Captain?

Your emergency fund should be like a well-stocked hold in case of storms. Aim to save enough to cover three to six months of living expenses. This will give you a buffer to weather financial storms without capsizing. Keep this fund in a place that's easily accessible but not too tempting to use for regular expenses, like a high-yield savings account.

Any advice for young sailors embarking on saving for big-ticket items?

Start early, young sailor, and be consistent. Whether for education, a car, a home, or emergencies, set a course and stick to it. Use the right tools, seek favorable winds in the form of scholarships or grants, and always keep an eye on the horizon. Remember, the sea of finances is vast, but with the proper preparation and a steady hand at the wheel, you can reach any destination you set your sights on.

The Captain's Guiding Light: Big-Ticket Purchases (Key Chapter Takeaways)

1. **Saving for College with 529 Plans and ESAs:** Utilize 529 College Savings Plans and Coverdell Education Savings Accounts for tax-advantaged saving towards future education costs, offering a structured way to finance higher education.

2. **Exploring Scholarships and Grants:** Actively seek out scholarships and grants, which provide non-repayable financial aid, reducing the need for student loans and easing the financial burden of education.

3. **Strategizing for Your First Car:** Plan for your first car by saving for a down payment, understanding auto loans, and considering the total costs of car ownership, including insurance, maintenance, and fuel.

4. **Homeownership Planning:** Navigate the process of buying a home by determining a budget, understanding mortgage options, saving for a down payment, and considering the long-term financial implications of homeownership.

5. **Building an Emergency Fund:** Establish an emergency fund with three to six months of living expenses to provide a financial safety net for unforeseen circumstances, ensuring it's easily accessible but not susceptible to impulsive use.

6. **The Role of Financial Planning in Big Purchases:** Emphasize the importance of proactive financial planning, budgeting, and saving when preparing for significant expenditures, highlighting the need for discipline and long-term vision.

7. **Utilizing Financial Tools and Resources:** Take advantage of various financial tools and resources, such as high-yield savings accounts for emergency funds and budgeting apps for tracking savings progress.

8. **Balancing Immediate Desires with Future Needs:** Balance the excitement of immediate purchases with the necessity of planning for future financial stability, considering the impact of current decisions on long-term goals.

9. **Adopting a Practical Approach to Financial Goals:** Encourage a practical and informed approach to financial planning, emphasizing research, comparison of options, and understanding the total cost of ownership for significant purchases.

10. **Preparing for Financial Independence:** Equip readers with the knowledge and skills to navigate significant financial decisions confidently, fostering a foundation for financial independence and responsible money management.

CHAPTER NINE

MONEY MINDSET - REWIRING YOUR FINANCIAL BLUEPRINT

I magine walking into a room filled with various musical instruments. A gleaming violin rests on one table, a shiny flute on another, and a majestic piano is in the corner. You're told you can create beautiful music, but there's a catch - you only know how to play one song and need to learn more. Daunting? Absolutely. Impossible? Not at all. With practice, patience, and a few discordant notes along the way, you could learn to play a variety of music. It's the same with our beliefs about money. They might be deeply ingrained, repeatedly playing the same tune in our heads, but we can change the melody with time, awareness, and effort.

In this chapter, we'll explore our money beliefs, understand how they impact our financial decisions, and discover strategies to rewrite any negative scripts. We'll create a new symphony of positive money beliefs, harmonizing our actions with our financial aspirations. Ready to conduct your financial orchestra? Let's dive into the first movement.

9.1 UNDERSTANDING YOUR MONEY BELIEFS

Identifying Your Money Beliefs: Unraveling the Melody

Our money beliefs are the underlying tune that guides our financial decisions and behaviors. They're like the sheet music for a song, setting the rhythm and melody. These beliefs are often formed in early childhood, influenced by our parents, experiences, and societal messages. They could be beliefs like

"Money doesn't grow on trees," "You have to work hard to earn money," or "Money is the root of all evil."

Take a moment to reflect on your beliefs about money. You could jot them down in a journal or ponder them. Think about phrases or attitudes about money you often heard growing up. Reflect on your past and present experiences with money. What beliefs are playing in the background of your financial life? Identifying these is the first step to understanding your money mindset.

How Money Beliefs Affect Your Finances: The Resounding Echo

Your money beliefs echo through your financial life, influencing how you spend, save, earn, and think about money. If you believe money is hard to come by, you might cling to it tightly, fearing spending or investing. On the other hand, if you think there's always more where that came from, you might spend freely, often beyond your means.

Imagine your money beliefs as the strings on a guitar. When you pluck a string, it vibrates, creating a specific note. Similarly, every time you make a financial decision, your money beliefs are being plucked, vibrating through your actions and creating the music of your financial reality.

Consider a belief like "Money is hard to earn." The effects of this belief could manifest as staying in a job you dislike. You fear you won't find another or not asking for a raise because you don't believe you'll get it. You're playing the same note repeatedly, creating a monotonous tune in your financial life.

Changing Negative Money Beliefs: Tuning Your Financial Instrument

Changing negative money beliefs is like tuning a musical instrument. It's about adjusting the strings, or beliefs, that are out of tune to create a more harmonious melody. It involves becoming aware of your negative beliefs, questioning their accuracy, and replacing them with positive, empowering ones.

Say you identify a belief like "I'm bad with money." First, question this belief. Is it true that you're bad with money, or did you make a few mistakes you've learned from? Then, replace it with a more positive belief, like "I'm capable of making wise financial decisions." Repetition is key here. The more you reinforce this new belief, the more it becomes part of your mental soundtrack.

Changing your money beliefs is more than just a one-and-done deal. It's an ongoing process, like tuning an instrument before each performance. But with each negative belief you change, you create a more empowering money mindset supporting your financial goals and dreams. The sweet notes of financial confidence and success are within your reach. So, keep tuning, practicing, and creating your unique financial symphony, one belief at a time.

Now that we've tuned our financial instruments and started creating a new melody, we'll move on to the next section:

creating a positive money mindset. This involves harnessing the power of positive thinking, visualization techniques, and affirmations to reinforce our new, empowering money beliefs. So, stay tuned for the next movement in our financial symphony. The music is just beginning to rise.

9.2 CREATING A POSITIVE MONEY MINDSET

The Power of Positive Thinking: Your Money Cheerleader

Let's kick off with the concept of positive thinking. Picture your thoughts as a cheerleading squad jumping, twirling, and chanting from the sidelines of your life. Positive thoughts cheer you on, filling you with energy, optimism, and confidence. They're like the cheerleaders doing a high-energy routine, pumping up the crowd and boosting team spirit.

The same applies to your money thoughts. Positive money thoughts, such as "I am capable of managing my finances" or "I am deserving of wealth," lift your financial spirit. They inspire you to take positive actions, like sticking to your budget or investing wisely. They're your money cheerleaders, chanting affirmations of financial success and prosperity.

Transforming your money thoughts from negative to positive can profoundly impact your financial life. It's like switching the cheerleading routine from a sluggish, lackluster performance to a lively, electrifying one. The energy shifts, the momentum increases, and suddenly, financial success seems within your reach.

Visualization Techniques: Picturing Prosperity

Next on the agenda is visualization, a powerful tool for creating a positive money mindset. Consider it like drawing a detailed mental map of your desired financial destination. It involves picturing your financial goals, imagining what it would feel like to achieve them, and visualizing the steps needed.

Say your goal is to be debt-free. Close your eyes and picture the moment you make your final loan payment. Imagine the joy and relief washing over you, the pride swelling in your chest, and the weight lifting off your shoulders. Visualize the steps you need to take to reach that goal, like making regular payments, cutting back on expenses, or earning extra income.

Visualization brings your financial goals to life, making them more tangible and attainable. It's like having a 3D map for your financial journey that you can see, touch, and explore. This vivid, sensory experience can motivate you to take action and make your financial dreams a reality.

Affirmations for Financial Success: Your Money Mantras

Finally, let's talk about affirmations, your personal money mantras. Affirmations are positive statements you repeat to yourself to reinforce your positive money beliefs and goals.

They're like catchy slogans on a billboard, grabbing your attention and sticking in your mind.

Affirmations work best when they're positive, present tense, and specific. For example, instead of saying, "I will be debt-free," say, "I am becoming debt-free by making smart financial choices daily." Repeat your affirmations daily, ideally out loud and in front of a mirror. Write them down and put them where you'll see them often.

Using affirmations can help rewire your brain for financial success. It's like updating the catchy slogans on your mental billboard, replacing outdated or negative messages with fresh, positive ones. These new messages then influence your thoughts, actions, and behaviors, steering you toward your financial goals.

Positive thinking, visualization, and affirmations are the keys to creating a positive money mindset. They're the tools that can tune your mind to the frequency of financial success, transforming discordant notes into a harmonious melody. The process may take time and practice, but with each positive thought, visualized goal, and spoken affirmation, you're composing a new money soundtrack that resonates with prosperity, abundance, and success. So, keep practicing, believing, and creating your wealth symphony, note by note, beat by beat.

9.3 RECOGNIZING AND OVERCOMING MONEY FEARS

Common Money Fears: Unmasking the Financial Bogeyman

Picture a closet filled with all sorts of objects. In the dark, the clothes look like lurking monsters, the hangers appear as spooky skeletons, and the old toys transform into creepy creatures. Our money fears are a lot like those imagined monsters in the closet. When left in the dark recesses of our minds, they take on a life of their own, seeming larger and scarier than they are.

Different people harbor different money fears. For some, it could be the fear of not having enough, worrying about running out of money, or facing financial hardship. Others might need help to avoid making mistakes with their money, like making a bad investment or falling into debt. Some people could have a fear of success, worrying that becoming wealthy could change them or their relationships with others.

These fears often lurk beneath the surface, influencing our financial decisions and behaviors without us even realizing it. They're like invisible puppeteers, pulling the strings of our financial life.

Strategies for Overcoming Money Fears: Turning on the Light

So, how do we overcome these money fears? It's all about turning on the light and seeing what's in the closet. The first step is to acknowledge your concerns. Write them down, say them out loud, or share them with a trusted friend or mentor. This simple act of acknowledgment is like flipping the light switch. It brings your fears into the open, stripping them of their power over you.

Next, challenge your fears. Is this fear rooted in reality or based on past experiences or assumptions? For example, if you fear making a bad investment, is it because you lack investment knowledge? If so, you can overcome this fear by educating yourself, seeking advice from financial advisors, or starting small with low-risk investments.

Another strategy is to reframe your fears. Instead of seeing them as obstacles, view them as opportunities for growth and learning. If you fear not having enough, use it as a motivation to save, budget, and plan for your financial future. If you fear making mistakes, remember that everyone makes mistakes and that they're often our best teachers.

Finally, practice positive affirmations. Counteract your fears with positive statements like "I am capable of making smart financial decisions," "I have the power to create financial abundance," or "I am worthy of financial success." Repeat these affirmations daily, and over time, they can help you reshape your money mindset and overcome your fears.

Building Financial Confidence: Becoming the Master of Your Money

Building financial confidence is like mastering your money puppet show. Instead of letting your fears pull your strings, you take control and direct your financial performance. Confidence comes from knowledge, experience, and positive thinking.

Knowledge is power, and this is especially true regarding finances. Educate yourself about money management, investing, and financial planning. Read books, attend workshops, listen to podcasts, or consult with a financial advisor. The more you learn, the more confident you'll become.

Experience is another great confidence builder. Start small, take one step at a time, and gradually take on more complex financial tasks. It's like learning to play a musical instrument. You start with straightforward notes, then move on to scales, and before you know it, you're playing entire melodies.

Finally, maintain a positive mindset. Celebrate your financial wins, no matter how small. Learn from your mistakes and view them as stepping stones, not stumbling blocks. Stay focused on your goals, but be flexible and willing to adjust your plans.

Building financial confidence takes time to happen. It's a process that involves growing your knowledge, gaining experience, and cultivating a positive mindset. With each step you take, you're becoming more and more the master of your financial puppet show. You're calling the shots, pulling the strings, and creating a performance that fits your financial goals and dreams. So, step into the spotlight, take a bow, and let the show begin.

9.4 EMPOWERMENT THROUGH FINANCIAL LITERACY

The Benefits of Financial Literacy: Unlocking a Treasure Trove

Think of financial literacy as a hidden treasure chest deep within a sunken ship. This treasure chest contains gems of knowledge, valuable wisdom nuggets, and golden confidence coins. The benefits of financial literacy are multiple, varied, and incredibly rewarding.

Financial literacy equips you with the skills to manage your money effectively. It's like having a compass in the vast ocean of finance, guiding you toward wise decisions and away from potential rough waters. You learn to budget, save, invest, and plan for the future. It's like finding a treasure map that leads you to financial stability and prosperity.

Secondly, financial literacy helps you avoid debt and financial traps. It's like having a strong anchor that prevents your ship from being swept away in a storm of high-interest loans or credit card debt.

Finally, financial literacy gives you the freedom to make informed choices. It's like having the wind in your sails, propelling you towards your financial goals quickly and confidently. You can choose the best savings account, insurance policy, and the most suitable investment options. You're in control, steering your financial ship.

Lifelong Learning and Financial Literacy: Navigating the Seas of Knowledge

Financial literacy, like any other skill, requires lifelong learning. The financial seascape is ever-changing, with new trends, tools, and technologies constantly emerging. Lifelong learning ensures you keep up with these changes and navigate the financial seas skillfully and confidently.

This continuous learning can take many forms. You might read books, attend workshops, listen to podcasts, or consult with financial advisors. Each learning experience adds a new tool to your financial toolkit, enhancing your abilities and expanding your horizons.

Lifelong financial literacy isn't about mastering every detail; it's about building a solid foundation to ask informed questions, seek guidance, and navigate the evolving world of finance with confidence and curiosity.

Using Financial Literacy for Empowerment: Steering Your Ship

At its core, financial literacy is a powerful tool for empowerment. It puts you at the helm of your financial ship, enabling you to steer your course toward the shores of monetary success.

With financial literacy, you're not at the mercy of the financial tides. You're not swayed by every passing fiscal fad or scared by every storm of economic uncertainty. Instead, you're the Captain of your financial ship, charting your course with knowledge, steering confidently, and navigating with skill.

Financial literacy empowers you to set and achieve your financial goals, whether buying a home, starting a business, retiring comfortably, or simply living within your means. It helps you build a solid financial foundation and create a prosperous financial future.

In the end, financial literacy is more than just understanding money. It's about understanding your relationship with money and using it as a tool to create the life you want. It's about taking charge of your financial destiny and steering your ship toward the shores of abundance, prosperity, and success.

As we bring this chapter to a close, remember the key message: financial literacy, like a trusted compass, is an empowerment tool. It's a beacon that guides us through personal finance's vast and often turbulent seas. By understanding our money beliefs, cultivating a positive money mindset, overcoming money fears, and embracing the power of financial literacy, we're not just surviving these seas - we're charting our course toward a brighter, prosperous future. So, let's keep this compass in hand, set our sights on the horizon, and sail forth with confidence and courage. The adventure continues, and the best is yet to come!

Ask the Captain

Captain, how do I change my deep-rooted negative beliefs about money?

Ahoy, navigator of fiscal seas! Changing deep-rooted beliefs is like adjusting your sails to catch a better wind. First, identify those beliefs. Are they tales of scarcity or fear? Then, challenge them - are they your beliefs or echoes of past voices? Replace them with affirmations of abundance and capability. Repeat these new beliefs like a shanty at sea until they become your new navigational stars.

Can positive thinking really impact my finances, Captain?

Indeed, young sailor! Positive thinking is like a favorable wind pushing your ship towards treasure-laden shores. It's about cultivating a mindset of abundance and possibilities. When you believe in your financial prowess and potential, you make decisions that align with prosperity and growth. Positive thinking is your compass towards a brighter financial horizon.

How can I overcome my fears about money, Captain?

To conquer your financial fears, you must face them like facing a storm at sea. Shine a light on these fears. Why do they lurk in your mind? Often, they're not as fearsome as they seem. Address them head-on, seek knowledge, and equip yourself with financial literacy. Remember, knowledge is your lighthouse in foggy financial waters.

What's the importance of financial literacy, Captain?

Financial literacy is your map and compass in the vast ocean of personal finance. It empowers you to navigate budgeting currents, investment winds, and the tides of saving and spending. With this knowledge, you're not adrift at the mercy of financial waves; you're charting your course toward a prosperous destination.

Any final words of wisdom for navigating my financial journey, Captain?

Stay curious, keep learning, and always be ready to adjust your sails. Your financial journey is ongoing – there will be calm seas and turbulent storms. Embrace each experience as an opportunity to grow. Keep your eyes on the horizon, your hands steady at the helm, and your heart open to the endless possibilities in the vast sea of personal finance. Fair winds and following seas on your journey, young sailor!

The Captain's Guiding Light: Money Mindset
(Key Chapter Takeaways)

1. **Identifying Personal Money Beliefs:** Recognize the underlying beliefs about money formed in childhood, which significantly impact financial decisions and behaviors.

2. **Impact of Money Beliefs on Finances:** Understand how deep-rooted money beliefs, whether positive or negative, shape financial habits like spending, saving, and investing.

3. **Changing Negative Money Beliefs:** Learn to challenge and replace negative money beliefs with positive, empowering ones through awareness and conscious effort.

4. **Embracing Positive Thinking:** Adopt positive thinking about money to foster a mindset of financial success, encouraging proactive and responsible financial behaviors.

5. **Visualization Techniques for Financial Goals:** Utilize visualization to make financial goals more tangible and attainable, enhancing motivation and clarity in achieving them.

6. **Using Affirmations for Financial Success:** Implement affirmations to reinforce positive money beliefs and goals, helping to rewire the brain for financial success.

7. **Recognizing and Overcoming Money Fears:** Address common financial fears by bringing them to

light, challenging their validity, and reframing them as opportunities for growth.

8. **Building Financial Confidence:** Develop financial confidence through knowledge acquisition, practical experience, and maintaining a positive mindset.

9. **Benefits of Financial Literacy:** Acknowledge the empowerment that comes from financial literacy, including effective money management, debt avoidance, and informed decision-making.

10. **Lifelong Learning in Financial Literacy:** Emphasize the importance of continuous learning in finance to keep up with evolving trends and to refine financial skills.

11. **Financial Literacy as a Tool for Empowerment:** Use financial literacy to take control of personal finances, setting and achieving goals, and navigating the financial landscape confidently.

12. **Empowerment through Knowledge and Skills:** Recognize that financial literacy empowers individuals to chart their own financial destiny, using money as a tool to create a fulfilling life.

Congratulations on Completing Your Journey!

"The sea is now behind you, but the lighthouse still stands, a beacon of knowledge in the world of personal finance."

You've completed "Essential Money Skills for Teens," and now you stand on the shore, equipped with the tools and knowledge to navigate your financial future.

Your Voice Can Shine a Light for Others

We'd love to hear about your journey:

- How has this book impacted your understanding of money?
- What lessons will you carry forward in your life?
- Would you recommend this book to other teens?

Your review on Amazon can serve as a guiding light for teens still navigating these waters. Help them find this lighthouse.

https://qrco.de/beYhae

Thank You for Being Part of Our Community!

Your insights and feedback are invaluable. Together, we can continue to illuminate the path for many more young navigators.

Remember, the lighthouse will always be here, shining a light on your path whenever you need guidance in your financial journey.

CONCLUSION - SETTING YOUR FINANCIAL SAILS

Congratulations, steadfast navigators of the fiscal waves! As our voyage through the monetary seas draws to a close, remember that your journey toward financial mastery is just beginning. With the compass of knowledge in hand and the charts of experience, however, you're well-equipped to sail toward the horizons of your dreams.

You've learned to read and harness the economic winds to propel you forward. You understand that the ebbs and flows of income, like the tides, are natural rhythms to be respected. You're ready to take the wheel and navigate the currents of budgeting, the swells of saving, and the storms of spending.

The treasure map laid out in these chapters, from the tranquil harbors of smart money habits to the tempestuous straits of credit and debt, is yours to keep. You've charted the reefs of risk and the vast oceans of opportunity that investing presents. And with the lighthouse of emergency funds shining brightly, you know you can weather any financial storm.

May the stars of ambition guide you and the winds of perseverance fill your sails as you embark on your lifelong odyssey of financial independence. Remember, the sea of finance is vast and full of wonders and perils alike, but you are the captain of your ship, and your destiny lies beyond the next wave.

So, young mariners, let's hoist the sails of ambition high! May your journey be prosperous, your bearings accurate, and your voyages fruitful. Here's to the seas ahead and you, the fearless navigators of your financial futures. Fair winds and following seas!

REFERENCES

1. Fidelity. (n.d.). Anatomy of a paycheck. Retrieved from https://www.fidelity.com/learning-center/personal-finance/anatomy-of-a-paycheck

2. Forbes Advisor. (n.d.). Gross pay vs. net pay. Retrieved from https://www.forbes.com/advisor/business/gross-pay-vs-net-pay/

3. Griffin and Co. (n.d.). How should a teenager fill out a W-4? Retrieved from https://griffinandco.com/how-should-a-teenager-fill-out-a-w-4/

4. Paychex. (n.d.). Benefits of direct deposit to employees and employers. Retrieved from https://www.paychex.com/articles/payroll-taxes/benefits-of-direct-deposit-to-employees-and-employers

5. The Ascent by The Motley Fool. (n.d.). 6 advantages and 4 disadvantages of online banking. Retrieved from https://www.fool.com/the-ascent/banks/articles/6-advantages-and-4-disadvantages-of-online-banking/

6. CNBC Select. (n.d.). Checking vs. savings. Retrieved from https://www.cnbc.com/select/checking-vs-savings/

7. Investopedia. (n.d.). Bank statement. Retrieved from https://www.investopedia.com/terms/b/bank-statement.asp

8. TODAY. (n.d.). Helping teens choose the right bank for college. Retrieved from https://www.today.com/parenting-guides/helping-teens-choose-right-bank-college-t177188

9. The College Pod. (n.d.). Budgeting for teens. Retrieved from https://thecollegepod.com/budgeting-for-teens/

10. SoFi. (n.d.). Types of budgeting methods. Retrieved from https://www.sofi.com/learn/content/types-of-budgeting-methods/

11. Kids Money. (n.d.). Money management apps for teens. Retrieved from https://www.kidsmoney.org/teens/money-management/apps/

12. Millennial Boss. (n.d.). Dave Ramsey cash envelope system. Retrieved from https://millennialboss.com/dave-ramsey-cash-envelope-system/

13. Investopedia. (n.d.). Compound interest. Retrieved from https://www.investopedia.com/terms/c/compoundinterest.asp

14. Consumer Financial Protection Bureau. (n.d.). Setting SMART savings goals. Retrieved from https://www.consumerfinance.gov/consumer-tools/educator-tools/youth-financial-education/teach/activities/setting-smart-savings-goal/

15. Business Insider. (n.d.). How to save money as a teenager. Retrieved from https://www.businessinsider.com/personal-finance/how-to-save-money-as-a-teenager

16. Modest Money. (n.d.). Importance of saving money from a young age. Retrieved from https://www.modestmoney.com/importance-saving-money-starting-young-age/

17. Sallie Mae. (n.d.). Credit card lessons for young adults. Retrieved from https://www.salliemae.com/blog/credit-card-lessons-for-young-adults/

18. Family Education. (n.d.). 14 credit card tips for teens: Understanding credit cards for teens. Retrieved from https://www.familyeducation.com/teens/values-responsibilities/jobs-money/14-credit-card-tips-for-teens-understanding-credit-cards-for-teens

19. Brookings. (n.d.). Revolving debts: Challenge to financial health and one way to help consumers pay it off. Retrieved from https://

www.brookings.edu/articles/revolving-debts-challenge-to-financial-health-and-one-way-to-help-consumers-pay-it-off/

20. Forbes. (2018). 10 ways young people can build a strong credit record. Retrieved from https://www.forbes.com/sites/forbesfinancecouncil/2018/01/23/10-ways-young-people-can-build-a-strong-credit-record/

21. Federal Student Aid. (n.d.). Federal vs. private loans. Retrieved from https://studentaid.gov/understand-aid/types/loans/federal-vs-private

22. National Association of Realtors. (n.d.). The impact of student loan debt. Retrieved from https://www.nar.realtor/research-and-statistics/research-reports/the-impact-of-student-loan-debt

23. Investopedia. (n.d.). 10 tips for managing your student loan debt. Retrieved from https://www.investopedia.com/articles/personal-finance/082115/10-tips-managing-your-student-loan-debt.asp

24. The College Investor. (n.d.). Best student loan alternatives. Retrieved from https://thecollegeinvestor.com/42315/best-student-loan-alternatives/

25. Investopedia. (n.d.). 10 investing concepts beginners need to learn. Retrieved from https://www.investopedia.com/10-investing-concepts-beginners-need-to-learn-5219500

26. Corporate Finance Institute. (n.d.). Stocks, bonds, and mutual funds. Retrieved from https://corporatefinanceinstitute.com/resources/career-map/sell-side/capital-markets/stocks-bonds-and-mutual-funds/

27. Investopedia. (n.d.). Risk tolerance. Retrieved from https://www.investopedia.com/terms/r/risktolerance.asp

28. Forbes. (2022). 5 apps to help teens start investing. Retrieved from https://www.forbes.com/sites/robertberger/2022/05/08/5-apps-to-help-teens-start-investing/

29. Saving for College. (n.d.). Coverdell ESA versus 529 plan. Retrieved from https://www.savingforcollege.com/article/coverdell-esa-versus-529-plan

30. 121 Financial Credit Union. (n.d.). How to buy your first car as a teenager. Retrieved from https://blog.121fcu.org/how-to-buy-your-first-car-as-a-teenager

31. Investopedia. (n.d.). First-time home buyer. Retrieved from https://www.investopedia.com/updates/first-time-home-buyer/

32. Mydoh. (n.d.). Emergency funds explained for teens. Retrieved from https://www.mydoh.ca/learn/money-101/building-credit/emergency-funds-explained-for-teens/

33. Synergy Eleven. (n.d.). Utilizing SMART Goals for business success: A comprehensive guide. Retrieved from https://synergy11.marketing/sculpting-your-success-the-art-of-setting-smart-goals-for-your-business/

34. VSECU. (n.d.). How money scripts influence financial behavior and how to change them. Retrieved from https://www.vsecu.com/blog/how-money-scripts-influence-financial-behavior-and-how-to-change-them/

35. Brian Tracy. (n.d.). How to develop a positive money mindset. Retrieved from https://www.briantracy.com/blog/financial-success/how-to-develop-a-positive-money-mindset/

36. gohenry. (n.d.). Common financial problems for teens & how to resolve them. Retrieved from https://www.gohenry.com/us/blog/financial-education/common-financial-problems-for-teens-how-to-resolve-them

37. National Financial Educators Council. (n.d.). Why is financial literacy important for youth. Retrieved from https://www.financialeducatorscouncil.org/why-is-financial-literacy-important-for-youth/

Made in United States
Troutdale, OR
11/30/2024